Moving from Shattered
to Strong

The 12 Steps to Becoming Well

From Intimacy Avoidance

For Christians

Matt Burton
Kevin Rose

Moving from
Shattered to Strong

THE 12 STEPS TO BECOMING WELL

From Intimacy Avoidance For Christians

MATT BURTON
KEVIN ROSE

Copyright © 2024 by Becoming Well, LLC

All rights reserved. No part of this book may be reproduced or transmitted in any form, or by any means, electronic or mechanical, including photocopying, recording, or by information storage or retrieval systems, without permission in writing from the copyright owner.

The views and opinions expressed in this book are those of the author, and do not necessarily reflect the official policy or position of Becoming Well, LLC

Published by Becoming Well, LLC

www.MyBecomingWell.com

Library of Congress Control Number

Paperback ISBN: 979-8-8693-9758-4

E-book ISBN: 979-8-8693-9759-1

Cover design by Monira

Printed in the United States of America

TABLE OF CONTENTS

Step		Page
1	We admitted we were powerless over our intimacy avoidance and that our lives had become unmanageable.	1
2	We came to believe that a power greater than ourselves could restore us to sanity.	23
3	We made a decision to turn our will and lives over to the care of God as we understand Him.	39
4	We made a searching and fearless moral inventory of ourselves.	57
5	We admitted to God, to ourselves, and to others the exact nature of our wrongs.	75
6	We were entirely ready to have God remove all these defects of character.	87
7	We humbly asked God to remove our shortcomings.	101
8	We made a list of all people we had harmed, and we became willing to make amends to them all.	113
9	We made direct amends to whomever possible, except when to do so would injure them or others.	125
10	We continue to take personal inventory and, when in the wrong, we promptly admit it.	137
11	We seek to improve contact with God through prayer and meditation, praying for knowledge of His will for our lives and the strength to carry it out.	157
12	Having had a spiritual awakening from our experience through the steps, we seek to share with others and practice our principles in all our relationships.	169

AUTHORS' NOTE

Although the publisher and the authors have made every effort to ensure that the information in this book was correct at press time and while this publication is designed to provide accurate information regarding the subject matter covered, the publisher and the authors assume no responsibility for errors, inaccuracies, omissions, or any other inconsistencies herein and hereby disclaim any liability to any party for any loss, damage, or disruption caused by errors or omissions, whether such errors or omissions result from negligence, accident, or any other cause.

This publication is meant as a source of valuable information for the reader. However, it is not meant as a substitute for direct expert assistance. If such a level of assistance is required, the services of a competent professional should be sought.

MATT AND LAURA BURTON

www.MyBecomingWell.com

INTRODUCTION

There are very few books, workbooks, etc. that address Intimacy Avoidants and help them break free from damage created through the many ways they self-protect, but this step book is one of them.

Though we here at Becoming Well don't view or believe that Intimacy Avoidance is an addiction, we do believe that the 12 steps are a very effective piece in your treatment and recovery puzzle. We view Intimacy Avoidance as an operating system that impacts and permeates every area of an IA's life, mostly and specifically in how they treat, think about, and engage (or not) with their primary romantic relationship. Though Intimacy Avoidance is not always exclusive to how IAs operate within their primary intimacy relationship, it is always centrally focused there. We IAs aren't bad people, but that doesn't change the fact that through our IA behaviors and attitudes, our IA operating system is shattering our partners, leaving them feeling rejected and unloved.

If you as an Intimacy Avoidant will embrace the work of recovery, it will be a transformational journey. Many come apprehensive, others skeptical. All of us come, if we're truthful, not "all in" with regards to doing whatever it takes to heal our hurts and the hurts we've caused others. One of the puzzle pieces of your recovery includes doing 12-step work.

The original version of the 12 steps was published in 1939 through Alcoholics Anonymous. Though started through A.A., they have since been replicated and used for many different addictions and other destructive coping strategies. From alcohol and drugs, to food and sex, to hoarding, gambling, and work, just to name a few.

We have created our version of both the steps themselves and questions in this workbook to dig deeper in an effort to help you experience and advance your healing from Intimacy Avoidance.

This step book will guide you methodically through each step as you work through them, either by yourself or – even better - with your Becoming Well Recovery workgroup or another recovery group you are involved in. Our hope for you is that you will find transformation both as an individual and within your relationship with your wounded partner.

Other materials available through Becoming Well, LLC and our Becoming Well Intensive Center in Tucson, AZ, may be helpful in your journey and are listed in the appendix of this book with a full list on our website. Virtual sessions for individuals and couples, Recovery Workgroups, Couples Private Intensives, and Guys Group Intensives (Becoming Well Bootcamp), as well as courses, books, and workbooks are also available nationwide and worldwide.

Please contact us for further information.

You can visit our website at

www.mybecomingwell.com

for access other resources for you and your partner

Becoming Well, LLC and Becoming Well Intensive Center

Phone number: 520-355-5322

Email address: Info@MyBecomingWell.com

STEP 1

Step 1 - We admitted we were powerless over our intimacy avoidance and that our lives had become unmanageable.

Memory Verse:

John 15: 5 MSG "I am the Vine, you are the branches. When you're joined with me and I with you, the relation is intimate and organic, the harvest is sure to be abundant. Separated, you can't produce a thing. Anyone who separates from me is deadwood, gathered up and thrown on the bonfire."

Goals

- **Be honest with yourself.**
  This is going to feel like a radical shift from how you once lived inside. You are no longer alone, and your struggle is something that you must share with others in order to heal.

Proverbs 12:22 MSG
God can't stomach liars; he loves the company of those who keep their word.

- **You are not in control.**
  You want to begin the practice of letting go of thinking that you have control over how you act in your intimacy avoidance or other destructive coping strategies. You will discover certain daily practices of surrender, prayer, and boundaries that will help you in the fight against slipping back into destructive patterns

Proverbs 25:28 MSG
A person without self-control is like a house with its doors and windows knocked out.

- **Share the burden of recovery.**
  We join a recovery group with the hope that we can get help. That help first and foremost comes with making phone calls to others in recovery. The goal is 6/7 calls minimum per week. If needed, call more, whenever you are triggered into acting out. We will and can help each other find a better way to live.

James 5:16 MSG
Admit your faults to one another and pray for each other so that you may be healed. The earnest prayer of a righteous man has great power and wonderful results.

Expectations

- This road of recovery requires routines, boundaries, and daily exercises take action. Having vision or desire to recover is not enough. Action, or believed behavior, is what your loved ones will see as evidence of your recovery, because action makes your vision of healing become possible.

1 John 3: 9, 10 MSG
People conceived and brought into life by God don't make a practice of sin. How could they? God's seed is deep within them, making them who they are. It's not in the nature of the God-born to practice and parade sin. The one who won't practice righteous ways isn't from God, nor is the one who won't love brother or sister. A simple test.

- Temptations will become less extreme the longer your sobriety lasts. Others in your recovery group will inspire you to press on, get back up, even after a slip. Listen to their guidance and put their feedback into more action.

1 John 3: 10,11 MSG
So now we can tell who is a child of God ... Whoever is living a life of sin and doesn't love his brother shows that he is not in God's family; 11 for the message to us from the beginning has been that we should love one another.

Hurdles

- Giving up control can feel counterintuitive.
  The 12 steps are built on the understanding that we cannot overcome our struggle with our own willpower, alone.

Ephesians 2:7-10 MSG
Now God has us where he wants us, with all the time in this world and the next to shower grace and kindness upon us in Christ Jesus. Saving is all his idea, and all his work. All we do is trust him enough to let him do it. It's God's gift from start to finish! We don't play the major role. If we did, we'd probably go around bragging that we'd done the whole thing!

No, we neither make nor save ourselves. God does both the making and saving. He creates each of us by Christ Jesus to join him in the work he does, the good work he has gotten ready for us to do, work we had better be doing.

- **You may reach desperation, a thirst, a drive inside you when you begin surrendering over the areas of your life that you need help in. Pride will get in the way.**

James 4:7-10 MSG
So let God work his will in you. Yell a loud no to the Devil and watch him make himself scarce. Say a quiet yes to God and he'll be there in no time. Quit dabbling in sin. Purify your inner life. Quit playing the field. Hit bottom, and cry your eyes out. The fun and games are over. Get serious, really serious. Get down on your knees before the Master; it's the only way you'll get on your feet.

- **Recovery is a marathon, not a sprint. Take everything one day at a time. Healing for yourself and loved ones will not happen in one day but is progressive, one day at a time.**

1 Corinthians 9: 24-27 MSG
You've all been to the stadium and seen the athletes race. Everyone runs; one wins. Run to win. All good athletes train hard. They do it for a gold medal that tarnishes and fades. You're after one that's gold eternally. I don't know about you, but I'm running hard for the finish line. I'm giving it everything I've got. No lazy living for me! I'm staying alert and in top condition. I'm not going to get caught napping, telling everyone else all about it and then missing out myself.

- **Remind yourself that you are worth it, you are worth healing, and you are worth the help others will give you through these desperate times.**

Luke 12:4-7 MSG
I'm speaking to you as dear friends. Don't be bluffed into silence or insincerity by the threats of religious bullies. True, they can kill you, but then what can they do? There's nothing they can do to your soul, your core being. Save your fear for God, who holds your entire life—body and soul—in his hands.

What's the price of two or three pet canaries? Some loose change, right? But God never overlooks a single one. And he pays even greater attention to you, down to the last detail—even numbering the hairs on your head! So don't be intimidated by all this bully talk. You're worth more than a million canaries.

Answer the following questions with an honest heart.

Share the answers that impact you the most when working with others in recovery.

"We" is important in this step to acknowledge that you are not alone and the only way to recover is together with support. Recovery is a team sport.

We have been in so many different groups/teams in our life. In what areas of your life have you needed a group in order to be successful? Does it make sense to be in a group in order to be in recovery? Why?

_____
_____
_____
_____
_____
_____
_____
_____

What groups or teams have you played a role in? Describe your roles.

_____
_____
_____
_____
_____
_____
_____
_____

Since stepping into recovery, what does it mean to be a part of a recovery group? What is the value of a recovery group?

_____
_____
_____
_____
_____

Name some challenges you may face when opening up to others for transparency and support.

_____
_____
_____
_____
_____
_____
_____

Name the types of groups you currently need in order to fully recover.

_____
_____
_____
_____
_____
_____
_____

Name the feelings associated with admitting your struggle to another person.

_____
_____
_____
_____
_____
_____
_____

What has kept you from admitting to yourself the seriousness of your struggle?

_____
_____
_____
_____
_____
_____
_____
_____

Name the specific behaviors or actions you are admitting you are powerless over. List the behaviors and the duration you've had these struggles for. Are you willing to admit and concede that without God's rule in your life, you have produced a harvest only worthy of a bonfire?

_____
_____
_____
_____
_____
_____
_____
_____
_____
_____
_____
_____

What consequences in life have led you to believe you are powerless?

_____
_____
_____
_____
_____
_____
_____
_____
_____

"Admitting we are powerless over our intimacy avoidance"

This part of Step 1 is crucial. Your operating system and ways of thinking have been formed and rehearsed since childhood. Accept it. Your unable to control with your own will the base desires of defensiveness, criticism, and/or anger to name a few.

(See Appendix for full list of Intimacy Avoidant behaviors)

What benefits do you see in admitting your powerlessness?

_____
_____
_____
_____
_____
_____
_____
_____

What do you plan to say to those who will try to diminish or minimize your intimacy avoidance?

_____
_____
_____
_____
_____
_____
_____

Name any evidence that comes to mind that points to a powerlessness over your struggle.

_____
_____
_____
_____
_____
_____
_____

Describe why those reasons above cause powerlessness.

_____
_____
_____
_____
_____
_____
_____

What is the purpose of admitting powerlessness for your recovery?

_____
_____
_____
_____
_____
_____
_____
_____

Name 3 feelings you have about being powerless.

1. _____

2. _____

3. _____

Describe the consequences your partner(s) have experienced from your powerlessness..

_____
_____
_____
_____
_____
_____
_____

Thinking about your life in general, what have you experienced that you have had no power over?

_____
_____
_____
_____
_____
_____
_____
_____
_____
_____
_____
_____
_____
_____
_____
_____
_____
_____
_____
_____
_____

"Our lives have become unmanageable."

You may want to deny this at times, that your life is unmanageable. However, the reality is that you are in recovery for very specific reasons. Owning those reasons is the first step in stepping out of the darkness of denial.

List 5 ways your life has become unmanageable and why.

1. _____
   _____

2. _____
   _____

3. _____
   _____

4. _____
   _____

5. _____
   _____

What costs has your struggle caused those you care about, besides monetary?

_____
_____
_____
_____
_____
_____
_____
_____
_____
_____
_____

Explain why you desire to recover.

_____
_____
_____
_____
_____
_____
_____

In what ways has pain affected your daily life?

_____
_____
_____
_____
_____
_____
_____
_____

Explain the suffering you have endured in your life. Do you feel that God was with you?

_____
_____
_____
_____
_____
_____
_____

Has your pain swayed your belief that God exists?

_____
_____
_____
_____
_____
_____
_____

Hiding can be detrimental to relationships. Name any secrets your family or you have hidden. How were these secrets hidden, and what did they look like?

_____
_____
_____
_____
_____
_____
_____

Name any fears you have that are associated with being honest with yourself and others.

_____
_____
_____
_____
_____
_____
_____

In what ways have you tried to avoid taking responsibility and/or being held accountable? Name anything that you have assigned blame to for your actions.

_____
_____
_____
_____
_____
_____
_____
_____

Name ideals you have that your current relationships or life lacks from your perspective.

_____
_____
_____
_____
_____
_____
_____
_____

Name how guilt and shame have come out of your intimacy avoidance.

_____
_____
_____
_____
_____
_____
_____
_____

How has your intimacy avoidance affected your education?

_____
_____
_____
_____
_____
_____
_____

How have you betrayed your character, morals, and values?

_____
_____
_____
_____
_____
_____
_____

How has your intimacy avoidance affected your belief system?

_____
_____
_____
_____
_____
_____
_____

THE 12 STEPS TO BECOMING WELL

How has your intimacy avoidance affected your finances?

_____
_____
_____
_____
_____
_____
_____

Name any erratic or risky behaviors you have acted on.

_____
_____
_____
_____
_____
_____
_____

Name the destruction your intimacy avoidance has caused with regards to others and yourself.

_____
_____
_____
_____
_____
_____
_____

Name the bottom lines that will define if you are sober" from acting out in your intimacy avoidance.

Step 1 Summary

List anything you hope to benefit from by completing Step 1.

_____
_____
_____
_____
_____
_____
_____
_____
_____
_____

Have you been honest throughout this step? Why or why not?

_____
_____
_____
_____
_____
_____
_____
_____
_____
_____

Explain why this step sets a foundation for your journey through the steps.

_____
_____
_____
_____
_____
_____
_____

Describe how it has felt to admit powerlessness over your struggle and that your life has become unmanageable.

_____
_____
_____
_____
_____
_____
_____

List what you have learned about yourself during Step 1.

_____
_____
_____
_____
_____
_____
_____

Create a goal that you can set today, and write in a safe place where you will see it, that can help you in your recovery and keep your serenity.

Memory Verse:

John 15:5-6 MSG
I am the Vine, you are the branches. When you're joined with me and I with you, the relation is intimate and organic, the harvest is sure to be abundant. Separated, you can't produce a thing. Anyone who separates from me is deadwood, gathered up and thrown on the bonfire.

Prayer:

Father,

Jesus is the Vine and I am a branch. Joined with Him, my relationship with You becomes intimate, personal, organic, and alive. I know when I think Your thoughts and do things Your way, I will produce an abundant harvest of wonderful fruit in my life. Separated from You, I can only produce decaying fruit filled with rotting matter. Living life apart from You only produces death and destruction, worthless poisonous byproducts only fit to be thrown into a bonfire, its ashes scattered to the winds.

I want to live an abundant life with a bountiful harvest of righteousness. When it's my time to leave this earth, I want my loved ones to say that I was a righteous person who got my act together and earnestly warned others not to travel down the path of destruction. I want my loved ones to know that from the time I became attached to Jesus, I was able to do all things through Christ. From that time onward, I was able to love You, Lord, and my family with all my being.

In Jesus' name, Amen.

Share your step summary with others in recovery. Be open to their feedback and what they have found in the importance of Step 1.

BECOMING WELL
STEP 2

Step 2 - We came to believe that a power greater than ourselves could restore us to sanity.

Memory Verse:

Jude 1:24-25 NLT "And now—all glory to Him who alone is God, who saves us through Jesus Christ our Lord; yes, splendor and majesty, all power and authority are His from the beginning; His they are and His they evermore shall be. And He is able to keep you from slipping and falling away, and to bring you, sinless and perfect, into His glorious presence with mighty shouts of everlasting joy. Amen."

Goals

- You begin exploring who God is and has been to you

Jeremiah 29: 12-14 MSG
"When you call on me, when you come and pray to me, I'll listen. When you come looking for me, you'll find me. Yes, when you get serious about finding me and want it more than anything else, I'll make sure you won't be disappointed." God's Decree

- This is a searching and reflection time of recovery. Your history with God is something that needs to be reflected upon.
- You will share this transformative time in step 2 through daily routines of accepting your feelings, anxieties, and fears in prayer and fellowship throughout your day.
- Building off of Step 1, there is a desperation for healing that you must carry with you throughout recovery. Therefore, a daily choice to believe healing is possible through God is a practice and action that you and you alone must choose.

Expectations

- **Daily spiritual practices are essential to recovery**

2 Timothy 3: 16-17 TLB
16 The whole Bible was given to us by inspiration from God and is useful to teach us what is true and to make us realize what is wrong in our lives; it straightens us out and helps us do what is right. 17 It is God's way of making us well prepared at every point, fully equipped to do good to everyone.

- AM, PM, and daily surrendering prayers are foundational parts of recovery. Expect to be required to check in with how these practices are going.
- Share all your heart with God. Bearing your thoughts, feelings, and temptations to God is essential as you emerge from your old habits of hiding.

Hurdles

- **Connecting to God can be mysterious and foreign**

Hebrews 11:6 MSG
It's impossible to please God apart from faith. And why? Because anyone who wants to approach God must believe both that he exists and that he cares enough to respond to those who seek him.

- Start with recovery, surrender, and gratitude prayers to God.
- Seek others in recovery for advice and help with where to start. Remember it is one day at a time, one prayer at a time, and one choice at a time.
- Prayer can feel awkward and shameful following the weight of relationship destruction. Remember that God hears you and wants healing for you. He doesn't want the avoidant behaviors that brought you into recovery to be the end of your story. He wants you to live a life of health and have a victorious ending to your story.

Answer the following questions with an honest heart.

Share the answers that impact you the most with others in recovery.

Name the areas of your life that have lost sanity. Insanity is doing the same thing over and over again and expecting different results. Share them with a group member this week.

_____
_____
_____
_____
_____
_____
_____

Describe what it would look like to be free from the above behaviors, and to change.

_____
_____
_____
_____
_____
_____
_____

Name any boundaries you have broken while acting out in your avoidance-related behavior.

_____
_____
_____
_____
_____
_____
_____

THE 12 STEPS TO BECOMING WELL

We say each week that we are 100% responsible for our actions in our life. Do you believe that? Who do you tend to place blame on?

_____
_____
_____
_____
_____
_____
_____
_____
_____
_____
_____
_____
_____

Name 5 traits of God.

1. _____
_____

2. _____
_____

3. _____
_____

4. _____
_____

5. _____
_____

Of those 5, are any of them new to you?

Describe your relationship with God. Name anything that has led you away from belief in God.

Describe a spiritual experience you've had or would like to have.

THE 12 STEPS TO BECOMING WELL

Describe how you have been defiant and/or strayed away from relying upon God.

_____
_____
_____
_____
_____
_____
_____

Name 3 recovery tools that have been helping you recover thus far. Explain why you believe they are helpful.

1. _____
_____
_____

2. _____
_____
_____

3. _____
_____
_____

What has someone shared that worked for them, which you are willing to apply in your own life?

_____
_____
_____
_____
_____
_____

Now, describe a specific tool someone else has used to build trust that you are willing to actively apply in your own relationships.

_____
_____
_____
_____
_____
_____
_____

Describe your experience with God's presence in your life. Name 3 daily habits that have cultivated the possibility of those experiences.

_____
_____
_____
_____
_____
_____

1. _____
_____

2. _____
_____

3. _____
_____

How can God help you recover? Describe your belief about His impact on your recovery.

_____
_____
_____
_____
_____
_____
_____

List areas of your life that can be restored with the aid of God. What will it look like to be restored in each area? Add this verse to the end of your paragraph. "He is able to keep me from slipping and falling away, and to bring me, sinless and perfect, into his glorious presence with mighty shouts of everlasting joy. Amen."

_____
_____
_____
_____
_____
_____

In the areas listed above, how has God already been providing restoration?

_____
_____
_____
_____
_____
_____

For your sanity, name 3 areas within your intimacy avoidance that you need God to bring restoration to.

1. _____
   _____
   _____

2. _____
   _____
   _____

3. _____
   _____
   _____

For the 3 you named above, provide behaviors someone will see in you that will provide evidence of your restoration.

_____
_____
_____
_____
_____
_____

How have your views of God changed over time?

_____
_____
_____
_____
_____

Name individuals who have influenced your attitude towards God. Share how each of them influenced you.

_____
_____
_____
_____
_____
_____
_____

With regards to your upbringing, what obstacles do you face in trusting God?

_____
_____
_____
_____
_____
_____
_____

Now, name any strengths your upbringing has given you.

_____
_____
_____
_____
_____
_____

Describe how God is working in your life right now.

_____
_____
_____
_____
_____
_____
_____
_____
_____
_____
_____
_____

How did your family of origin view the act of asking for help from others?

_____
_____
_____
_____
_____
_____
_____
_____
_____
_____
_____
_____

List 3 questions or doubts about the existence of God. Share these questions with others in recovery. Ask someone in recovery to answer these questions and record their answers here.

1. _____
   _____
   _____

2. _____
   _____
   _____

3. _____
   _____
   _____

Step 2 Summary

Congratulations on completing your second step.

Now, write a summary of what you have learned about yourself in the space below.

Include:

- **What you have learned about yourself,**
- **your intimacy avoidance, and**
- **what you must choose to do in order to stay in recovery.**

Describe what the Bible means by God's splendor, majesty, power, and authority.

Describe how Step 2 has been a choice to believe in the help that God can give to us.

_____

_____

_____

_____

_____

_____

_____

_____

_____

_____

_____

_____

_____

_____

_____

_____

_____

_____

THE 12 STEPS TO BECOMING WELL

Memory Verse:

Jude 1:24-25 NLT
And now—all glory to Him who alone is God, who saves us through Jesus Christ our Lord; yes, splendor and majesty, all power and authority are His from the beginning; His they are and His they evermore shall be. And He is able to keep you from slipping and falling away, and to bring you, sinless and perfect, into His glorious presence with mighty shouts of everlasting joy. Amen.

Prayer:

Father,

You alone are God! You saved me through Jesus Christ, my Lord. To You belongs all of the splendor and majesty. To You belongs all power and authority. I repent of ardently worshiping Your creation and handing over to them all the splendor, majesty, power and authority that belongs to You. I thank You for Your forgiveness and mercy. I am but dust and I am grateful that You understand my weaknesses.

Empower me with Your grace. The grace that keeps me from slipping and falling away. The grace that presents me sinless and perfect to You, to my loved ones and to my community. I thank You for loving me so much, that it pleases You to celebrate me and bring me into Your glorious presence with mighty shouts of everlasting joy! You alone are God and worthy of ALL my praise. You alone are splendid, majestic, powerful and have full authority in my life.

In Jesus' name I pray, Amen.

Share your step summary with others in recovery. Be open to their feedback and what they have found in the importance of Step 2.

BECOMING WELL
STEP 3

Step 3 - We made a decision to turn our will and lives over to the care of God as we understand Him.

Memory Verse:

Deuteronomy 31: 7-8 MSG "Be strong. Take courage. You will enter the land with this people, this land that God promised their ancestors that he'd give them. You will make them the proud possessors of it. God is striding ahead of you. He's right there with you. He won't let you down; He won't leave you. Don't be intimidated. Don't worry."

Goals

- This is a decision, not made in one day or in one minute, but every day, every prayer, and every phone-call cry for help as we live a different life from the one we lived before.

James 1:12 MSG
12 Anyone who meets a testing challenge head-on and manages to stick it out is mighty fortunate. For such persons loyally in love with God, the reward is life and more life.

- We need to make and revise boundaries to keep us sober in our recovery whenever triggering situations arise.

Psalm 16:5-11 MSG
My choice is you, God, first and only. And now I find I'm your choice! You set me up with a house and yard. And then you made me your heir! The wise counsel God gives when I'm awake is confirmed by my sleeping heart. Day and night I'll stick with God; I've got a good thing going and I'm not letting go. I'm happy from the inside out, and from the outside in, I'm firmly formed. You canceled my ticket to hell— that's not my destination! Now you've got my feet on the life path, all radiant from the shining of your face. Ever since you took my hand, I'm on the right way.

- We live in fellowship, turning over our lives to God. This will involve honest assessment of the areas in our lives that may be unhealthy.

Psalm 16: 1-3 MSG
Keep me safe, O God, I've run for dear life to you. I say to God, "Be my Lord! Without you, nothing makes sense. And these God-chosen lives all around— what splendid friends they make!

Expectations

- **Freedom is found in full surrender.**

1 Peter 5:5,6 TLB
And all of you serve each other with humble spirits, for God gives special blessings to those who are humble, but sets himself against those who are proud. If you will humble yourselves under the mighty hand of God, in his good time he will lift you up.

- **Our weaknesses are where we begin turning our lives over in order to receive healing and newfound strength.**
- **This is when we get into the details of where we need to turn over control. Whether finances or whatever way you withhold, you will need to examine anything and everything that you idolize and obsess over that takes the place of God in your heart.**
- **Sharing any anxiety or hesitation with those further in recovery will aid you in step 3.**

Hurdles

- **Turning over our lives could mean changing where we spend our time, money, and attention. The truths God will begin revealing to you about unhealthy habits, relationships, and entertainments can be hard to accept.**

Psalm 101: 1-3 MSG
My theme song is God's love and justice, and I'm singing it right to you, GOD. I'm finding my way down the road of right living, but how long before you show up? I'm doing the very best I can, and I'm doing it at home, where it counts. I refuse to take a second look at corrupting people and degrading things. I reject made-in-Canaan gods, stay clear of contamination.

- **Trusting in God is easier said than done. This is a daily practice, and if done with honesty and submission, it will be a painful and rewarding battle won with God by your side.**

Psalm 101:3-5 MSG
I reject made-in-Canaan gods, stay clear of contamination. The crooked in heart keep their distance; I refuse to shake hands with those who plan evil. I put a gag on the gossip who bad-mouths his neighbor; I can't stand arrogance.

- Moving on without fully submitting your life and will implies you aren't ready to move into Step 4. So slow down. One day at a time, seek God in prayer and turn to others for help. Remember, you are worth it!

Psalm 101:6-8 MSG
But I have my eye on salt-of-the-earth people—they're the ones I want working with me; Men and women on the straight and narrow—these are the ones I want at my side.

But no one who traffics in lies gets a job with me; I have no patience with liars. I've rounded up all the wicked like cattle and herded them right out of the country.

I purged God's city of all who make a business of evil.

Answer the following questions with an honest heart.

Share the answers that impact you the most with others in recovery

Name the rock bottoms that have brought you to a point of desperation to turn your will over to God

_____
_____
_____
_____
_____
_____
_____
_____
_____
_____
_____

List all the intimacy avoidant ways you are choosing to surrender your own power and will over. Incorporate Psalm 101 MSG version in the list.

_____
_____
_____
_____
_____
_____
_____

Describe when and why you made a choice to turn your life and will over to God in the past.

_____
_____
_____
_____
_____
_____
_____

Describe what desperation means in regard to your recovery.

_____
_____
_____
_____
_____
_____

In reflection of the times when you've felt desperate for recovery in the past, how is this moment in time different? Why?

_____
_____
_____
_____
_____
_____
_____

What changes are you beginning to experience as a result of turning your life and will over to God?

_____
_____
_____
_____
_____
_____
_____

What moments or events coalesced into this decision to turn your life and will over to God for recovery?

_____
_____
_____
_____
_____
_____

THE 12 STEPS TO BECOMING WELL

List the areas in your life for which you are hesitant to give control to God. Identify feelings for each.

_____
_____
_____
_____
_____
_____
_____

What steps will you take to surrender control over the areas listed above to God?

_____
_____
_____
_____
_____
_____
_____

List daily habits you are currently implementing in order to give over your will.

_____
_____
_____
_____
_____
_____
_____

Name evidence of God's care for you, which you have seen since turning turned your life over to Him.

_____
_____
_____
_____
_____
_____
_____
_____
_____
_____
_____

Which areas of your life are you willing to have God take authority over?

_____
_____
_____
_____
_____
_____
_____
_____
_____
_____

Exercise:

Contact 3 people from recovery in the next 2 weeks. Ask them what it looked like for them to turn their will over to God, along with the areas that may have been challenging at first to surrender control over.

Person #1: _____

What they said:

_____
_____
_____
_____
_____
_____
_____
_____
_____

Person #2: _____

What they said:

_____
_____
_____
_____
_____
_____
_____
_____

Person #3: _____

What they said:

_____
_____
_____
_____
_____
_____
_____
_____
_____
_____

Use the Feelings Wheel to list specific feelings you are having related to trusting God with your life (see appendix).

_____
_____
_____
_____
_____
_____
_____
_____
_____
_____

Name the ways you have tried to control and make up for your struggles on your own.

Name the frustrations and doubts you hold about yourself and God.

Aside from the intimacy avoidance that brought you into recovery, have there been any revelations about additional struggles in your life?

Our caregivers set an example for how we begin viewing God in our lives. List relationships in your life in which someone was supposed to care for you but didn't. How did those relationships impact your views of God?

_____
_____
_____
_____
_____
_____
_____

Do you typically see others as being better or worse than you? How does God view you?

_____
_____
_____
_____
_____
_____
_____

Describe how you have typically measured yourself as good or bad.

_____
_____
_____
_____
_____
_____

Describe any doubts you have about God accepting you. Name anything you have done that has created that doubt. Copy Deuteronomy 31: 7-8 MSG and put your name in this verse.

_____
_____
_____
_____
_____
_____
_____
_____
_____
_____
_____

How are you working towards opening up to others in recovery on a regular basis?

_____
_____
_____
_____
_____
_____
_____
_____
_____

Exercise:

There are red light behaviors, yellow light behaviors, and green light behaviors.

- Red light actions are when you withhold or avoid intimacy, or do other relationship-destroying behaviors.
- Yellow light actions are on the edge, when you're heading towards withholding or avoiding intimacy, or other relationship-destroying behaviors.
- Green lights are safe actions.

Create your Red, Yellow, and Green light list.

Red:

_____
_____
_____
_____
_____
_____
_____
_____
_____
_____

Yellow:

_____
_____
_____
_____
_____
_____
_____

THE 12 STEPS TO BECOMING WELL

Green:

Step 3 Summary

Congratulations on completing your third step.

Now, write a summary of what you have learned about yourself in the space below.

Include:

- **What you have learned about yourself,**
- **your intimacy avoidance, and**
- **what you must choose in order to rely upon God's will and power in your life.**

Copy Psalm 101 and put your name in those verses.

Describe how **Step 3** has been a choice to believe in the help that God can give to us.

_____
_____
_____
_____
_____
_____
_____
_____
_____
_____
_____
_____
_____
_____
_____
_____
_____

THE 12 STEPS TO BECOMING WELL

Memory Verse:

Deuteronomy 31: 7-8 MSG
"Be strong. Take courage. You will enter the land with this people, this land that God promised their ancestors that He'd give them. You will make them the proud possessors of it. God is striding ahead of you. He's right there with you. He won't let you down; He won't leave you. Don't be intimidated. Don't worry."

Prayer:

Father,

By Your grace, I am STRONG. By Your grace, I take COURAGE. I will enter the land with Your people and my loved ones, the land that You promised me! You will make me a proud possessor of my land, my home, my life. You are striding ahead of me taking care of all the obstacles and challenges.

You are right there with me! You won't let me down! You won't leave me! I will not be intimidated by the challenge set before me. I will not worry but make the right choices, both small and large.

In Jesus' name, Amen.

Share your step summary with others in recovery. Be open to their feedback and what they have found in the importance of Step 3.

STEP 4

Step 4 - We made a searching and fearless moral inventory of ourselves.

Memory Verse:

2 Corinthians 8:21 NIV "For we are taking pains to do what is right, not only in the eyes of the Lord but also in the eyes of man."

Goals

- This is where honesty gets put into action. We document and reflect on our past in:

  - Intimacy Avoidant harms done to me
  - Intimacy Avoidant harms done to others
  - Intimacy Avoidant tendencies toward others

Proverbs 11: 3-6 MSG
The integrity of the honest keeps them on track; the deviousness of crooks brings them to ruin. A thick bankroll is no help when life falls apart, but a principled life can stand up to the worst. Moral character makes for smooth traveling; an evil life is a hard life. Good character is the best insurance; crooks get trapped in their sinful lust.

- We reflect upon how we acted out or withheld, why we acted out or withheld, and the feelings that we associate with the actions that we committed or that were done to us.

Titus 2:12 MSG
We're being shown how to turn our backs on a godless, indulgent life, and how to take on a God-filled, God-honoring life.

Expectations

- **By listing out our history, we begin searching for full honesty with God and others.**
- **We may need to add to our inventory as time passes.**
- **It is not necessary to disclose your inventory. Talking to a recovery coach, a therapist, or trusted spiritual leader will create a safe space to vent feelings associated with revisiting the past.**
- **Disclosure in a marriage may be necessary, BUT be sure to create plans for such a disclosure with appropriate planning and guidance, using individual and couples recovery counseling or coaching.**
- **Becoming Well providers are an option for help with this process. We can create a safe space for such a disclosure to be accomplished with the least amount of pain possible.**
- **We have experience and are certified and trained, but we also know firsthand from our own history of recovery that disclosure can look many different ways for different couples. The key is to be honest to the extent that it will help your partner feel safe.**

Titus 2: 12-15 MSG
We're being shown how to turn our backs on a godless, indulgent life, and how to take on a God-filled, God-honoring life. This new life is starting right now, and is whetting our appetites for the glorious day when our great God and Savior, Jesus Christ, appears. He offered himself as a sacrifice to free us from a dark, rebellious life into this good, pure life, making us a people he can be proud of, energetic in goodness.

(Titus the Pastor/Leader) Tell them all this. Build up their courage, and discipline them if they get out of line. You're in charge. Don't let anyone put you down.

Hurdles

- **Emotions are raw when listing out your history of destruction from Intimacy Avoidance. At this point, leaning on God and recovery partners will be essential to overcome the inevitable grief you will feel while recording your inventory.**
  - **Have a list of people to call handy whenever you're working through your inventory.**

- **You may feel broken and not worthy of healing while listing out the pain you have caused others.**

- **Return to the foundation of Steps 1, 2, and 3, and remind yourself that God wants nothing less than to free you from your broken ways of thinking.**

- **Adjust your daily recovery prayers to grieve the pain and seek God for the strength to live a life in full surrender.**

- **Seek others in recovery who have experienced the freedom from completing a thorough Step 4 inventory. This step can and should be thorough. Take your time, because it will be worth the effort.**

Psalm 51 MSG
Generous in love—God, give grace! Huge in mercy—wipe out my bad record. Scrub away my guilt, soak out my sins in your laundry. I know how bad I've been; my sins are staring me down. You're the One I've violated, and you've seen it all, seen the full extent of my evil. You have all the facts before you; whatever you decide about me is fair. I've been out of step with you for a long time, in the wrong since before I was born. What you're after is truth from the inside out. Enter me, then; conceive a new, true life. Soak me in your laundry and I'll come out clean, scrub me and I'll have a snow-white life. Tune me in to foot-tapping songs, set these once-broken bones to dancing. Don't look too close for blemishes, give me a clean bill of health.

God, make a fresh start in me, shape a Genesis week from the chaos of my life. Don't throw me out with the trash, or fail to breathe holiness in me. Bring me back from gray exile, put a fresh wind in my sails! Give me a job teaching rebels your ways so the lost can find their way home. Commute my death sentence, God, my salvation God, and I'll sing anthems to your life-giving ways. Unbutton my lips, dear God; I'll let loose with your praise. Going through the motions doesn't please you, a flawless performance is nothing to you. I learned God-worship when my pride was shattered. Heart-shattered lives ready for love don't for a moment escape God's notice.

Answer the following questions with an honest heart. Share the answers that impact you the most with others in recovery.

Intimacy Avoidant Inventory

***Not every table will need to be filled out for everyone. Nevertheless, reflect on all IA acting-out behavior to consider and possibly discover where you may have acted out.

When do you avoid intimate moments with others?	When did you first begin avoiding and withdrawing from others?	How have you avoided connection with others?
How have your gut reactions been pushing others away from you?	What specific circumstances trigger you to act out in IA in an unmanageably painful way towards others?	What are some of the recurring patterns in your reactions and reasons?
Who was involved in your IA acting-out?	What groups/teams were you a part of in which you acted out in IA?	

IA (Intimacy Avoidance) Checklist

You will dig deep into these in your inventory below. For each that applies to you, you will need to consider all your actions in regard to these avoidance tendencies. Choose 10 from the list of 44 to complete your inventory with.

40 ways to be IA (Intimacy Avoidant)

1. **Marked lack of empathy.**
2. **Oversensitivity to criticism or perceives criticism when there is none.**
3. **Low emotional expression and bandwidth.**
4. **Jumps to conclusions.**
5. **Contempt for self/others.**
6. **Sabotages emotional connectedness.**
7. **Reactive rather than Proactive in relationships.**
8. **Spiritually independent or disengaged.**
9. **Requires Hoop Jumping.**
10. **Defensiveness.**
11. **Prideful and/or Unteachable.**
12. **Blame-shifting.**
13. **Offends from the victim position.**

14. Suspicious of partner.
15. Gaslighting.
16. Stonewalling/Punishing through anger.
17. Frequent lying.
18. Avoids taking responsibility for actions.
19. Breadcrumbing or Love Bombing.
20. Emotionally disengaged.
21. Feelings are facts.
22. Poor self reflection.
23. Self-preoccupation.
24. Labels themselves and others.
25. Focuses on the faults of others.
26. Objectification.
27. Poor demeanor.
28. Sexually disconnected or avoidant.
29. Sexual gratification outside of committed relationship.
30. Inability to handle conflict productively.
31. All-or-nothing thinking (black-and-white thinking).
32. An intense need to be right.
33. Easily offended.
34. Maximization and minimization of faults and/or good deeds.
35. Constant activity that disrupts relational connection.
36. Plays the victim.
37. Hero or Zero.
38. I did it my way.
39. Cynical Script.
40. Married but Unloved.

THE 12 STEPS TO BECOMING WELL

1_____

Subject	What Happened	My Reaction (Door A)	My Reason
I acted in this avoidance behavior toward_____ *List the people, places, or groups*	The situation/ circumstance tied to this IA behavior: _____ *Tell the story(ies) of when you withdrawal with ____*	The response I had was_____ *Describe your feelings and behaviors*	I acted the way I did out of_____ *Name the nature of your reasons (ex: fear, selfishness, loneliness, prideful, control, comfort...)*

*Use additional paper if needed to record more

FROM INTIMACY AVOIDANCE FOR CHRISTIANS

2_____

Subject	What Happened	My Reaction (Door A)	My Reason
I acted in this avoidance behavior toward_____ *List the people, places, or groups*	The situation/ circumstance tied to this IA behavior: _____ *Tell the story(ies) of when you withdrawal with _____*	The response I had was_____ *Describe your feelings and behaviors*	I acted the way I did out of_____ *Name the nature of your reasons (ex: fear, selfishness, loneliness, prideful, control, comfort...)*

*Use additional paper if needed to record more

3_____

Subject	What Happened	My Reaction (Door A)	My Reason
I acted in this avoidance behavior toward_____ ***List the people, places, or groups***	The situation/circumstance tied to this IA behavior: _____ ***Tell the story(ies) of when you withdrawal with _____***	The response I had was_____ ***Describe your feelings and behaviors***	I acted the way I did out of_____ ***Name the nature of your reasons (ex: fear, selfishness, loneliness, prideful, control, comfort...)***

*Use additional paper if needed to record more

4 _____

Subject	What Happened	My Reaction (Door A)	My Reason
I acted in this avoidance behavior toward_____ *List the people, places, or groups*	The situation/ circumstance tied to this IA behavior: _____ *Tell the story(ies) of when you withdrawal with _____*	The response I had was_____ *Describe your feelings and behaviors*	I acted the way I did out of_____ *Name the nature of your reasons (ex: fear, selfishness, loneliness, prideful, control, comfort...)*

*Use additional paper if needed to record more

5_____

Subject	What Happened	My Reaction (Door A)	My Reason
I acted in this avoidance behavior toward_____ *List the people, places, or groups*	The situation/ circumstance tied to this IA behavior: _____ *Tell the story(ies) of when you withdrawal with _____*	The response I had was_____ *Describe your feelings and behaviors*	I acted the way I did out of_____ *Name the nature of your reasons (ex: fear, selfishness, loneliness, prideful, control, comfort...)*

*Use additional paper if needed to record more

6_____

Subject	What Happened	My Reaction (Door A)	My Reason
I acted in this avoidance behavior toward_____ *List the people, places, or groups*	The situation/ circumstance tied to this IA behavior: _____ *Tell the story(ies) of when you withdrawal with ____*	The response I had was_____ *Describe your feelings and behaviors*	I acted the way I did out of_____ *Name the nature of your reasons (ex: fear, selfishness, loneliness, prideful, control, comfort...)*

*Use additional paper if needed to record more

7_____

Subject	What Happened	My Reaction (Door A)	My Reason
I acted in this avoidance behavior toward_____ *List the people, places, or groups*	The situation/ circumstance tied to this IA behavior: _____ *Tell the story(ies) of when you withdrawal with _____*	The response I had was_____ *Describe your feelings and behaviors*	I acted the way I did out of_____ *Name the nature of your reasons (ex: fear, selfishness, loneliness, prideful, control, comfort...)*

*Use additional paper if needed to record more

8 _____

Subject	What Happened	My Reaction (Door A)	My Reason
I acted in this avoidance behavior toward_____ *List the people, places, or groups*	The situation/ circumstance tied to this IA behavior: _____ *Tell the story(ies) of when you withdrawal with _____*	The response I had was_____ *Describe your feelings and behaviors*	I acted the way I did out of_____ *Name the nature of your reasons (ex: fear, selfishness, loneliness, prideful, control, comfort...)*

*Use additional paper if needed to record more

9_____

Subject	What Happened	My Reaction (Door A)	My Reason
I acted in this avoidance behavior toward_____ *List the people, places, or groups*	The situation/ circumstance tied to this IA behavior: _____ *Tell the story(ies) of when you withdrawal with _____*	The response I had was_____ *Describe your feelings and behaviors*	I acted the way I did out of_____ *Name the nature of your reasons (ex: fear, selfishness, loneliness, prideful, control, comfort...)*

*Use additional paper if needed to record more

10 _____

Subject	What Happened	My Reaction (Door A)	My Reason
I acted in this avoidance behavior toward_____ *List the people, places, or groups*	The situation/ circumstance tied to this IA behavior: _____ *Tell the story(ies) of when you withdrawal with _____*	The response I had was_____ *Describe your feelings and behaviors*	I acted the way I did out of_____ *Name the nature of your reasons (ex: fear, selfishness, loneliness, prideful, control, comfort...)*

*Use additional paper if needed to record more

Step 4 Summary

Congratulations on completing your fourth step.

- **Now, write a summary of what you have learned about yourself in the space below. Include:**

  - **What parts of your inventory were hardest/easiest to reflect on?**
  - **Patterns in your Intimacy Avoidant behaviors**
  - **Specific "Natures" you tend to resort to in IA (last column)**

Consider what these behaviors look like in God's eyes and in man's eyes.

_____
_____
_____
_____
_____
_____
_____
_____
_____
_____
_____
_____
_____
_____
_____
_____
_____

Memory Verse:

2 Corinthians 8:21 NIV
For we are taking pains to do what is right, not only in the eyes of the Lord but also in the eyes of man.

Prayer:

Father,

I am taking great pains to do what is right. I will do what is right in Your sight. I will meet all of Your requirements with humility and grace. I will also do what is right in the eyes of man, and especially in the eyes of my partner and loved ones. I will do it in the attitude of humility and by Your grace.

In Jesus' name, Amen.

Share your step summary with others in recovery. Be open to their feedback and what they have found in the importance of Step 4.

BECOMING WELL
STEP 5

Step 5 - We admitted to God, to ourselves, and to others the exact nature of our wrongs.

Memory Verse:

1 James 1:8-10 MSG: "If we claim that we're free of sin, we're only fooling ourselves. A claim like that is errant nonsense. On the other hand, if we admit our sins—simply come clean about them—He won't let us down; He'll be true to Himself. He'll forgive our sins and purge us of all wrongdoing. If we claim that we've never sinned, we out-and-out contradict God—make a liar out of Him. A claim like that only shows off our ignorance of God."

Goals

- This is where you become fully vulnerable, an open book, about your history to God and to others.

Ephesians 2: 1-5 MSG
It wasn't so long ago that you were mired in that old stagnant life of sin. You let the world, which doesn't know the first thing about living, tell you how to live. You filled your lungs with polluted unbelief, and then exhaled disobedience. We all did it, all of us doing what we felt like doing, when we felt like doing it, all of us in the same boat. It's a wonder God didn't lose his temper and do away with the whole lot of us. Instead, immense in mercy and with an incredible love, he embraced us. He took our sin-dead lives and made us alive in Christ.

- You will share your inventory with a recovery partner.
- Disclosure to your significant other may be overdue and needed, so you will need to seek help in how to give a full disclosure. Becoming Well can help with that, or any other trained recovery coach or counselor who specializes in disclosure delivery.

- **Admitting to God is an ongoing process. Accepting the nature of your wrongs is an intimate process that starts with daily honesty with your God.**

1 John 1:9 MSG
If we admit our sins—simply come clean about them—he won't let us down; he'll be true to himself. He'll forgive our sins and purge us of all wrongdoing.

- **Aim to fit time into your daily prayers and recovery work to speak light to your inventory, sharing it with God.**

Proverbs 8:17 KJV
I love them that love me; and those that seek me early shall find me.

Expectations

- **Sharing your story will be freeing and uplifting. You will see a huge stride in momentum in your recovery during this step.**

  - **Keeping this momentum is important to be able to complete the 12-step process.**

- **The peace you feel from being open and honest, for maybe the first time ever, can be an exciting rush.**

  - **Therefore, that freedom is very personal. Others may not be feeling the freedom you are. Remaining under the pain they may still be experiencing is expected.**

- **Whatever it is that you may have said to yourself, "I will take this to my grave" is exactly what you need to share with another and confess to God. Your healing and recovery depend on it.**

Hurdles

- **Fear and secrecy can get in the way of being vulnerable and honest. The lies that your pain and addiction will tell you can get in the way of your recovery and healing.**
- **As mentioned before, your freedom and relief in being completely honest may be viewed negatively by loved ones, especially any you have betrayed.**

  - **Be prepared to use tools to give space for their feelings of pain that persist or flare up. It is understandable for them to still feel pain.**
  - **If you need help understanding the other person's feelings, consult with a Becoming Well provider or other trained professionals.**

- **Always, always remember: you are worth recovery.**

1 John 1: 5-7 MSG
God is light, pure light; there's not a trace of darkness in him. If we claim that we experience a shared life with him and continue to stumble around in the dark, we're obviously lying through our teeth—we're not living what we claim. But if we walk in the light, God himself being the light, we also experience a shared life with one another, as the sacrificed blood of Jesus, God's Son, purges all our sin.

Answer the following questions with an honest heart.

Share the answers that impact you the most with others in recovery.

List any reasons why it is difficult to admit your wrongs. Share your reasons with others in recovery that have completed their Step 5.

_____
_____
_____
_____
_____
_____
_____

List the most memorable times in your past when you wronged another with your behavior.

_____
_____
_____
_____
_____
_____
_____

When you share your inventory with another, what expectations do you have of them?

_____
_____
_____
_____
_____
_____

Contact your recovery partner and schedule a time to share your inventory with them. Write the name of the person and the date and time you have scheduled to complete this.

_____
_____
_____
_____
_____
_____

After sharing with your Step 5 recovery partner, is there anything you didn't share about? If so, list the items you have not shared from your inventory and prepare to disclose them to your recovery partner as soon as possible. Being honest and open about your past is essential to your healing and recovery.

_____
_____
_____
_____
_____
_____

Describe your experience and feelings about admitting your wrongs to another.

_____
_____
_____
_____
_____
_____
_____

What have you learned about yourself through the process of telling your story to another?

_____
_____
_____
_____
_____
_____
_____

List the most meaningful exercises, practices, and experiences you have had in recovery thus far.

_____
_____
_____
_____
_____
_____
_____

THE 12 STEPS TO BECOMING WELL

List the challenging parts of recovery for you thus far.

_____
_____
_____
_____
_____
_____
_____

Would your family consider you to be humble? Why or why not?

_____
_____
_____
_____
_____
_____
_____

List the standards of living that allowed you to keep your Intimacy Avoidance in secret and that enabled it to survive.

_____
_____
_____
_____
_____
_____
_____

Name the feelings you have that keep you from being honest with yourself and others. Share these with a recovery partner.

_____
_____
_____
_____
_____
_____
_____

Are you fearful, ignorant, or prideful about sharing your struggles in recovery? If so, explain the reasons for each. Copy Proverbs 8:17 and personalize this verse.

_____
_____
_____
_____
_____
_____
_____

List specific patterns of lies from your inventory that have kept you isolated in your struggle.

_____
_____
_____
_____
_____
_____

After sharing with your recovery partner, list what you have learned regarding fear, trust, and acceptance.

_____
_____
_____
_____
_____
_____
_____

Name any differences between sharing your struggle with a person and with God.

_____
_____
_____
_____
_____
_____
_____

What will you plan on doing if you forget to share something in your inventory with your recovery partner?

_____
_____
_____
_____
_____
_____

Step 5 Summary

Congratulations on completing your fifth step.

- **Now, write a summary of what you have learned about yourself in the space below. Include:**
  - **What parts of your inventory were hardest/easiest to reflect on**
  - **Patterns in your IA behaviors**
  - **Specific "Natures" you tend to resort to in IA (last column)**

_____
_____
_____
_____
_____
_____
_____
_____
_____
_____
_____
_____
_____
_____
_____
_____
_____
_____
_____

THE 12 STEPS TO BECOMING WELL

Memory Verse:

1 James 1:8-10 MSG
If we claim that we're free of sin, we're only fooling ourselves. A claim like that is errant nonsense. On the other hand, if we admit our sins—simply come clean about them—He won't let us down; He'll be true to Himself. He'll forgive our sins and purge us of all wrongdoing. If we claim that we've never sinned, we out-and-out contradict God—make a liar out of Him. A claim like that only shows off our ignorance of God.

Prayer:

Father,

I admit all of my sins. I decided to come clean. You won't let me down. You are true to Yourself. You will forgive me of all my sins and purge me of all wrongdoing. Thank you for embracing me and making me Your child.

In Jesus' name, Amen.

Share your step summary with others in recovery. Be open to their feedback and what they have found in the importance of Step 5.

BECOMING WELL — STEP 6

Step 6 - We were entirely ready to have God remove all these defects of character.

Memory Verse:

2 Chronicles 7:14 MSG: "My people, my God-defined people, respond by humbling themselves, praying, seeking my presence, and turning their backs on their wicked lives. I'll be there ready for you: I'll listen from heaven, forgive their sins, and restore their land to health."

Goals

- Here's where we become ready for change.
  - It may include giving up habits, attitudes, or ways of thinking.
  - Whatever the defect is that you identified in your inventory, your target in this step is to prepare your heart for putting those behaviors behind you.
- Be open to feedback and reflection.
  - If your actions are still a reflection of your defects, then you will need to be open to humility.
  - In this process, you may need to add to and record an ongoing inventory.

Romans 12: 1, 2 MSG
So here's what I want you to do, God helping you: Take your everyday, ordinary life—your sleeping, eating, going-to-work, and walking-around life—and place it before God as an offering. Embracing what God does for you is the best thing you can do for him. Don't become so well-adjusted to your culture that you fit into it without even thinking. Instead, fix your attention on God. You'll be changed from the inside out. Readily recognize what he wants from you, and quickly respond to it. Unlike the culture around you, always dragging you down to its level of immaturity, God brings the best out of you, develops well-formed maturity in you.

Expectations

- This step will consolidate and summarize the defects you identified in your inventory.
- You will need to share this process of summing up your flaws with others in recovery.
- Healing involves simply saying out loud that you are ready. Pray regularly, AM, PM, and throughout the day to prepare for God to help you remove your character defects.

Romans 12: 9-12 MSG
Love from the center of who you are; don't fake it. Run for dear life from evil; hold on for dear life to good. Be good friends who love deeply; practice playing second fiddle. Don't burn out; keep yourselves fueled and aflame. Be alert servants of the Master, cheerfully expectant. Don't quit in hard times; pray all the harder.

Hurdles

- Being ready for defects to be removed may involve removing unhealthy habits, pastimes, or relationships from your life.
  - Help from others in recovery and God will reveal aspects of your life that need to be removed.
  - Removing your defects can be painful, like going into surgery. Exercises like appreciation and resignation letters can help with letting things go from your past.
- Seek guidance from others in recovery and hear how they became ready for God to remove their character defects.
- Keeping true to daily submission, this is a one-day-at-a-time process, so let go and let God and others help you prepare to begin moving past your character defects and into a new life.

Proverbs 3: 1-12 MSG
Good friend, don't forget all I've taught you; take to heart my commands. They'll help you live a long, long time, a long life lived full and well. Don't lose your grip on Love and Loyalty. Tie them around your neck; carve their initials on your heart. Earn a reputation for living well in God's eyes and the eyes of the people. Trust God from the bottom of your heart; don't try to figure out everything on your own. Listen for God's voice in everything you do, everywhere you go; he's the one who will keep you on track.

Don't assume that you know it all. Run to God! Run from evil! Your body will glow with health, your very bones will vibrate with life! Honor God with everything you own; give him the first and the best. Your barns will burst, your wine vats will brim over. But don't, dear friend, resent God's discipline; don't sulk under his loving correction. It's the child he loves that God corrects; a father's delight is behind all this.

Answer the following questions with an honest heart.

Share the answers that impact you the most with others in recovery.

List events in your life where you were motivated to act and change.

_____
_____
_____
_____
_____
_____
_____
_____

Describe God's role in your recovery thus far through Steps 1-5 in a short paragraph. Include your feelings, habits, and relationship towards God. Also, include why you believe you have needed God throughout the recovery process.

_____
_____
_____
_____
_____
_____
_____

THE 12 STEPS TO BECOMING WELL

If your struggles and character defects were removed, what feelings would you have?

List out the character defects you have identified from inventory (Step 4) in regards to your IA behaviors. Then, write a short paragraph explaining what life would be like without them and what life would be like if you continued acting out in them.	
Defect	Paragraph

Name anything you are unwilling to do or change in order to gain freedom from your struggle.

_____
_____
_____
_____
_____
_____
_____

Name any desires, passions, pleasures, or loves that you are not yet ready to turn away from.

_____
_____
_____
_____
_____
_____
_____

Reflect on any behavior patterns or coping mechanisms from your Step 4 inventory and list out some people, places, or decisions that tend to lead you toward those behaviors.

_____
_____
_____
_____
_____
_____

What decisions can you make today to turn away from your past IA behaviors? Define Biblical humility and write how that would look like in your life.

_____
_____
_____
_____
_____
_____
_____

Name any desires you fear will not be satisfied if you turn them over to God. Ask yourself what God will do for you if you humble yourself before Him.

_____
_____
_____
_____
_____
_____
_____

Describe what life would be like if your IA behaviors no longer directed you in response to hardship and conflict.

_____
_____
_____
_____
_____
_____

THE 12 STEPS TO BECOMING WELL

Name the changes you need to make that you know are or will be the most difficult in your recovery.

_____
_____
_____
_____
_____
_____
_____

List any desires that God has already begun changing.

_____
_____
_____
_____
_____
_____
_____

Then, list any new desires since joining recovery.

_____
_____
_____
_____
_____
_____
_____

List any old patterns and ways you have already begun turning from.

_____
_____
_____
_____
_____
_____
_____

Then, name new habits and practices you are developing.

_____
_____
_____
_____
_____
_____
_____

Name any relationships that need to change in your life in order for you to recover. Specify the ones that need to end, change, or continue to grow.

_____
_____
_____
_____
_____
_____
_____

Willing and Help Needed Exercise:

<u>Left Column:</u> List out the specific character defects you are currently willing to turn over to God. Pray over each one this week and share them with a recovery partner.

<u>Right Column:</u> List out the character defects you need help letting go of. Pray over these on your own and with a recovery partner, asking specifically for God's help to turn them over.

Character Defects I am Willing to Turn Over to God	Defects I Need to Help Turning Over to God

Affirmations Exercise:

Name a self-affirmation about your character every day for the next 7 days.

Being able to recognize and see the new you in recovery brings confidence and a new identity. Then, write a prayer of gratitude for these characteristics you see in yourself.

Day	Self-Affirmation	Prayer of Gratitude
1		
2		
3		
4		
5		
6		
7		

Step 6 Summary

Congratulations on completing your sixth step.

- **Now, write a summary of what you have learned about yourself in the space below. Include:**

    - **What character defects are you willing to have God remove?**
    - **What areas of your life need to change for their removal?**
    - **What self-affirmation(s) comforted you about who God has created you to be?**

Memory Verse:

2 Chronicles 7:14 MSG
my people, my God-defined people, respond by humbling themselves, praying, seeking my presence, and turning their backs on their wicked lives. I'll be there ready for you: I'll listen from heaven, forgive their sins, and restore their land to health.

Prayer:

Father,

I am your child, one of your God-defined people. I am responding to Your love by humbling myself, by praying, by seeking Your presence and turning my back on my wicked ways. I choose to live my life in a godly manner. According to Your promise, You will be ready for me. You will listen to my humble cry from heaven. You will forgive and cleanse me of all my sins. You will restore my land, my sphere of influence and all that I am in charge of, back to health. I thank You for watching over Your word to perform it and bringing it to pass.

In Jesus' name, Amen.

Share your step summary with others in recovery. Be open to their feedback and what they have found in the importance of Step 6.

BECOMING WELL — STEP 7

Step 7 - We humbly asked God to remove our shortcomings.

Memory Verse:

1 Corinthians 10:13 TLB: "But remember this—the wrong desires that come into your life aren't anything new and different. Many others have faced exactly the same problems before you. And no temptation is irresistible. You can trust God to keep the temptation from becoming so strong that you can't stand up against it, for He has promised this and will do what he says. He will show you how to escape temptation's power so that you can bear up patiently against it."

Goals

- This is a process of practicing full surrender.
  - Create prayers to God asking Him to remove your character defects.
  - Imagine what life would be like without your struggle
- Ongoing Inventory needs to be taken daily
  - When a defect arises, return to asking God for its removal

2 Peter 2:9 MSG
So God knows how to rescue the godly from evil trials. And he knows how to hold the feet of the wicked to the fire until Judgment Day.

2 Timothy 4: 17, 18 ESV
But the Lord stood by me and strengthened me, so that through me the message might be fully proclaimed and all the Gentiles might hear it. So I was rescued from the lion's mouth. The Lord will rescue me from every evil deed and bring me safely into his heavenly kingdom. To him be the glory forever and ever. Amen.

Expectations

- Full recovery involves sharing your struggles with others. This is a key way to involve others and God in the process of removal.

Hebrews 10:23, 24 EASY
We know that we can trust God to do the things that He has promised. So we must continue to expect those things. We must tell other people that we trust God. We should not stop doing that. We should think about how we can help one another. We want everyone to show love to each other. We want everyone to do good things to help one another.

- A key to success is:
  - Trusting fully in God.
  - Believing that God can help.

Proverbs 3:5-8 ESV
Trust in the LORD with all your heart, and do not lean on your own understanding. In all your ways acknowledge him, and he will make straight paths. Be not wise in your own eyes; fear the LORD, and turn away from evil. It will heal your flesh and refresh your bones.

- Strong emotion may rush out when you're imagining the removal of your defect.
- The feeling of desperation is good.
- Thirsting for a new way of living, provided by God, is a gift.

Matthew 5:6 ESV
Blessed are those who hunger and thirst for righteousness, for they shall be satisfied.

Hurdles

- This is the place where you've passed the halfway mark through the 12 steps, so don't give up!
- Half efforts now will yield half results later.
- Practicing forgiving yourself, one defect at a time, and asking for their removal one at a time is how you begin to love yourself and in turn become able to love others fully.

Deuteronomy 7:9 MSG
Know this: God, your God, is God indeed, a God you can depend upon. He keeps his covenant of loyal love with those who love him and observe his commandments for a thousand generations.

Answer the following questions with an honest heart.

Share the answers that impact you the most with others in recovery.

List out experiences in which you have displayed humility.

_____
_____
_____
_____
_____
_____
_____

Name the feelings you had when you displayed a humble attitude.

_____
_____
_____
_____
_____
_____
_____

Name anything that you have asked God for and in turn received.

_____
_____
_____
_____
_____

Reflect upon your character defects from Step 6 and list out the ones you would like to ask God to remove. Write out 1 Corinthians 10:13 and put your name in this verse.

_____
_____
_____
_____
_____
_____
_____
_____

Describe God's character as you ask for your defects to be removed. If you have experienced those characteristics from God in the past, describe how.

_____
_____
_____
_____
_____
_____
_____
_____

What are your expectations when asking things of God? Write out Deuteronomy 7:9 and put your name in this verse.

_____
_____
_____
_____
_____
_____

Ask 3 others in recovery who have gone through Step 7 and record their experiences here.

Person #1: _____

What they said:

_____
_____
_____
_____
_____
_____
_____
_____
_____
_____
_____
_____

Person #2: _____

What they said:

_____
_____
_____
_____
_____
_____
_____
_____
_____
_____

THE 12 STEPS TO BECOMING WELL

Person #3: _____

What they said:

_____
_____
_____
_____
_____
_____
_____
_____
_____

Use the feelings wheel to list specific feelings you are having in relation to trusting God.

_____
_____
_____
_____
_____
_____
_____
_____
_____
_____

List out each character defect from Step 6 below.

Then, next to each, write a prayer to God asking for their removal.

Pray for strength to surrender the defects over, giving God control over them, and the wisdom to make healthy decisions to move towards recovery.

Give God a sense of prioritization over which is to be removed first, and then honestly rank them in their order of importance and urgency. This process may take days. If you don't see a clear ranking, continue to pray over them and bring up the struggle to a recovery partner.

Be prepared to share the top 2 prayers you have written in your Step Summary.

Defect	Prayer

Name ways you have tried to change on your own with no success.

Write a personal mission statement for your life from this day forward.

Would you be satisfied if God removed the defect(s) that brought you to recovery? Why or why not?

FROM INTIMACY AVOIDANCE FOR CHRISTIANS

Name 2 actions you can take to strengthen your relationship with God.

1. _____
_____
_____
_____

2. _____
_____
_____

Exercise: Name actions in daily, weekly, and monthly practices that you are taking to become:	
Honest	
Selfless	
Considerate	
Courageous	

Step 7 Summary

Congratulations on completing your seventh step.

- **Now, write a summary of what you have learned about yourself in the space below. Include:**

  - **Two prayers from the exercise above and describe your feelings while putting them into practice.**
  - **Any fears or feelings associated with God removing your defects.**

Memory Verse:

1 Corinthians 10:13 TLB
But remember this—the wrong desires that come into your life aren't anything new and different. Many others have faced exactly the same problems before you. And no temptation is irresistible. You can trust God to keep the temptation from becoming so strong that you can't stand up against it, for He has promised this and will do what He says. He will show you how to escape temptation's power so that you can bear up patiently against it.

Prayer:

Father,

Your word tells me that these wrong desires that I experience aren't anything new or different. Many others have faced exactly the same problems before I did. BUT, You are telling me that NO TEMPTATION is irresistible!

I can trust You to keep this temptation from becoming so strong that I CAN STAND UP AGAINST IT!!! This is Your promise and You will do what You say You will do! You will show me how to escape temptation's power so I can bear up patiently against it and be a victor and not a victim. Thank You, Father!

In Jesus' name, Amen!

Share your step summary with others in recovery. Be open to their feedback and what they have found in the importance of Step 7.

BECOMING WELL
STEP 8

Step 8 - We made a list of all people we had harmed, and we became willing to make amends to them all.

Memory Verse:

Numbers 5:5, 6 MSG: "God spoke to Moses: 'Tell the People of Israel, When a man or woman commits any sin, the person has broken trust with God, is guilty, and must confess the sin. Full compensation… must be made to whoever was wronged.'"

Goals

- Reflect on all the people and organizations you wronged from your inventory.
- If you think of someone or some group you have missed, list them out as well in this step.
- Become clear on what making amends is and what it isn't.
- Have multiple discussions with those who have completed amends before. Take notes on how it went for them.
- Become willing by God's strength, not your own. Surrender personal judgements and seek to forgive prior to entering an amends.

Luke 19:1-10 MSG
Then Jesus entered and walked through Jericho. There was a man there, his name Zacchaeus, the head taxman and quite rich. He wanted desperately to see Jesus, but the crowd was in his way—he was a short man and couldn't see over the crowd. So he ran on ahead and climbed up in a sycamore tree so he could see Jesus when he came by. When Jesus got to the tree, he looked up and said, "Zacchaeus, hurry down. Today is my day to be a guest in your home." Zacchaeus scrambled out of the tree, hardly believing his good luck, delighted to take Jesus home with him.

Everyone who saw the incident was indignant and grumped, "What business does he have getting cozy with this crook?" Zacchaeus just stood there, a little stunned. He stammered apologetically, "Master, I give away half my income to the poor—and if I'm caught cheating, I pay four times the damages." Jesus said, "Today is salvation day in this home! Here he is: Zacchaeus, son of Abraham! For the Son of Man came to find and restore the lost."

Zacchaeus compensated, made amends for the people he robbed from and Jesus said that salvation entered his life that day!

Expectations

- Amends Is NOT...
  - Expecting forgiveness from the person you harmed.
  - About sharing reasons for your struggles.
  - Placing blame for your struggles on traumas you've endured.
  - Expecting the other party to own their wrongs.

- Amends Is...
  - Communicating your faults and taking responsibility.
  - Recognizing the pain you have caused.
  - Asking for forgiveness.

- Becoming willing is another process involving prayer.
- Forgiving others for their wrongs frees you to be able to love them from this day on, whether they want to reconcile a relationship with you or not.

Leviticus 5: 17-19 MSG
"If anyone sins by breaking any of the commandments of GOD which must not be broken, but without being aware of it at the time, the moment he does realize his guilt he is held responsible. He is to bring to the priest a ram without any defect, assessed at the value of the Compensation-Offering. "Thus the priest will make atonement for him for his error that he was unaware of and he's forgiven. It is a Compensation -Offering; he was surely guilty before God."

Luke 3: 8-14 MSG
"Being a child of Abraham is neither here nor there—children of Abraham are a dime a dozen. God can make children from stones if he wants. What counts is your life. Is it green and flourishing? Because if it's deadwood, it goes on the fire."

The crowd asked him, "Then what are we supposed to do?"
"If you have two coats, give one away," he said. "Do the same with your food."
Tax men also came to be baptized and said, "Teacher, what should we do?"
He told them, "No more extortion—collect only what is required by law."
Soldiers asked him, "And what should we do?"
He told them, "No harassment, no blackmail—and be content with your rations."

Hurdles

- **Feelings can get in the way of making your amends**

    - Anger, resentment, pride, malice... basically anything that breeds a defensive or entitled stance
    - Unforgiveness is at the root of your judgment towards someone. Forgiving them says, "I am handing their judgment over to God."

- Becoming willing to make amends can look different depending on if a face-to-face amends will harm someone. Being willing to give a face-to-face amends is best, but Step 9 will explore other options.
- Owning up to your role in causing others pain can be frightening. Asking God for the courage you need can be added to your daily prayers. Discuss such hesitancies with someone in recovery. Remember, you are worth it to God and your loved ones to own your mistakes.

Matthew 5:23-26 MSG
This is how I want you to conduct yourself in these matters. If you enter your place of worship and, about to make an offering, you suddenly remember a grudge a friend has against you, abandon your offering, leave immediately, go to this friend and make things right. Then and only then, come back and work things out with God. Or say you're out on the street and an old enemy accosts you. Don't lose a minute. Make the first move; make things right with him. After all, if you leave the first move to him, knowing his track record, you're likely to end up in court, maybe even jail. If that happens, you won't get out without a stiff fine.

Answer the following questions with an honest heart.

Share the answers that impact you the most with others in recovery.

Reflect upon your progress in recovery and the 12-Step process.

In Steps 1-3 you admitted your need for God and have placed your trust in that belief.

Then, in Step 4, you created an inventory of all the harms you have done and suffered from others.

Most recently, in Steps 5-7, you identified the nature of your wrongs and asked God for the removal of your defects.

Now you must reflect on those in your inventory whom you have harmed and become willing to make amends to them. It is only now, in the progress of your recovery, that you are capable of recognizing the pain and harm you have caused in complete detail and honesty.

List out the people, places, and organizations you have wronged in the first column.

In the second column, name the pain in general that you have caused.

People, places, and organizations	Pain, wrong, or betrayal caused

Continued	
People, places, and organizations	Pain, wrong, or betrayal caused

THE 12 STEPS TO BECOMING WELL

Name the primary feelings you felt while making your list.

_____
_____
_____
_____
_____
_____
_____

In becoming willing to make amends, we must understand what amends is and isn't.

Amends is/isn't:

- **Is taking responsibility for your role you've played**
- **Is not others' responsibilities**
- **Is identifying the hurt you've caused another**
- **Is not denying or excusing the hurt others have caused you**
- **Should not be avoided if someone is unaware of your activity**
- **Does not free you from potential consequences for your actions**
- **Is doing your part to repair your wrongs in the relationship, whether or not others take ownership of their own needs for recovery**
- **Is not reconciliation**
- **Is not necessarily done face-to-face when an amends may hurt another**

False Motives – the purpose of making your amends is:

- **Not to draw out an amends from another**
- **Not to make someone like or accept you**
- **Not to be heard or express your own hurt**
- **Not to hurt another out of demonstrating your perspective or defense**
- **Not to punish or shame yourself**

Describe in your own words what it would look like to be willing to make amends to another.

List out the names of people, places, or organizations you are willing/not willing to make amends with and why for each.

Then, write a prayer for strength through a will other than your own (Step 3 principle) to help you become willing to make amends.

Write a prayer for each person in your list whom you're hesitant to make amends with. Share this prayer with someone in recovery who has done Steps 8 and 9.

Then, record their contact information once you become willing to make amends.

Note: It is understandable to be hesitant in Step 8 for a time in order to become willing to make amends.

People, places, and organizations	Why not willing	Prayer and Contact Information

Describe your struggle with guilt and shame related to your infidelity-related behaviors.

Who have you falsely blamed? List them and explain.

What exercises or daily practices have you obtained in recovery that can help you accept yourself for the harms you have done to others and yourself?

Step 8 Summary

Congratulations on completing your eighth step.

- **Now, write a summary of what you have learned about yourself in the space below. Include:**
  - **Explain what amends is and isn't in your own words.**
  - **Name any person, place, or organization you are not yet willing to make amends with and your reason why.**

Write Numbers 5:5, 6 and insert your name, sin, and those you have wronged into this verse.

"Tell the People of Israel, When a [I] commit _____(name sin), [I have] broken trust with God, [am] guilty, and must confess _____(name sin). Full compensation … must be made to _____ [whom I have] wronged."

_____
_____
_____
_____
_____
_____
_____
_____
_____
_____
_____
_____
_____
_____
_____
_____

Memory Verse:

Numbers 5:5, 6 MSG
God spoke to Moses: "Tell the People of Israel, When a man or woman commits any sin, the person has broken trust with God, is guilty, and must confess the sin. Full compensation… must be made to whoever was wronged."

Prayer:

Father,

I now understand that every thought, word, and action carries value. When I am tempted to do something ungodly and destructive, give me the grace to intelligently evaluate the emotional, physical and spiritual value of that action. Your word gives me the knowledge and wisdom to understand that I must make compensation for what I harm, kill, steal or destroy.

Romans 13 says don't run up debts, except for the huge debt of love we owe each other. When I love others, I complete what the law has been after all along. The Code of the Law is this: Love other people as well as you do yourself. I can't go wrong when I love others. I will never run up a debt from any transgression that I can't ever really repay. Only the blood of Jesus can do that. I will not mock God. I will not harm, steal, kill or destroy in any way, shape, or form what Jesus came to save and bring life to.

In Jesus' name I pray, Amen.

Share your step summary with others in recovery. Be open to their feedback and what they have found in the importance of Step 8.

STEP 9

Step 9 - We made direct amends to whomever possible, except when to do so would injure them or others.

Memory Verse:

2 Samuel 12: 13, 22-25 MSG: Then David confessed to Nathan, "I've sinned against God"... [then] David went and comforted his wife...

Context:

"While the child was alive," he said, "I fasted and wept, thinking God might have mercy on me and the child would live. But now that he's dead, why fast? Can I bring him back now? I can go to him, but he can't come to me." David went and comforted his wife Bathsheba. And when he slept with her, they conceived a son. When he was born they named him Solomon. God had a special love for him and sent word by Nathan the prophet that God wanted him named Jedidiah (God's Beloved).

Goals

- Decide who you can deliver an amends face-to-face to.
  - This will be a hard decision and will depend on whether or not giving a face-to-face amends will harm the person you have wronged and whether or not they will want to receive your amends.
  - Counsel from others who have given their amends before is essential.
- Write amends to every person or group from your inventory whom you have harmed. This is a healing process for you.
- You will need to read your rough drafts to someone experienced in giving amends and make revisions.
- And finally, give your amends.

John 15:9-15 MSG
I've loved you the way my Father has loved me. Make yourselves at home in my love. If you keep my commands, you'll remain intimately at home in my love. That's what I've done—kept my Father's commands and made myself at home in his love.

I've told you these things for a purpose: that my joy might be your joy, and your joy wholly mature. This is my command: Love one another the way I loved you. This is the very best way to love. Put your life on the line for your friends. You are my friends when you do the things I command you. I'm no longer calling you servants because servants don't understand what their master is thinking and planning. No, I've called you friends because I've let you in on everything I've heard from the Father.

We must put our lives on the line for all. We are friends with God when we follow His example and do what He commands of us to do. We no longer selfishly entitle ourselves to take what we want when we want it but give of ourselves willingly.

Expectations

- So here it is, a recipe for amends letter writing, RUT-ABC
    - R - Recognize the Wrong
    - U - Understanding the Hurt
    - T - Take Responsibility
    - A - Ask for Forgiveness
    - BC - Behavior Change

- You will use your inventory to direct much of this process. There is a lot of explanation for what Amends is, what it isn't, and what each part of RUT-ABC should look like.

- This process can take a substantial amount of time. It is understandable. Practice delivering the amends that are more challenging and prepare for the possible feelings the receiver may have.

- Take enough time reflecting on what amends is, what amends isn't, false motives giving and amends.

Galatians 5:22, 23 MSG
But what happens when we live God's way? He brings gifts into our lives, much the same way that fruit appears in an orchard—things like affection for others, exuberance about life, serenity. We develop a willingness to stick with things, a sense of compassion in the heart, and a conviction that a basic holiness permeates things and people. We find ourselves involved in loyal commitments, not needing to force our way in life, able to marshal and direct our energies wisely.

Hurdles

- Their feelings may be centered on pain and anger.

  - Expect to stand under their feelings.
  - You will need to prepare for how they may react to you asking for forgiveness. If emotions are high, preparing some diffusing strategies may be needed. Seek counsel on such strategies from others more experienced at giving amends.

- God will be your strength through the amends-writing process and when you're giving the amends.

  - Dependence upon God will be tested.
  - You are worth owning your defects and how they have caused pain to others. Remember that giving your amends and moving towards reconciliation is going to strengthen your recovery and your relationship with God.

Galatians 5:11-12 MSG
Not only that — count yourselves blessed every time people put you down or throw you out or speak lies about you to discredit me. What it means is that the truth is too close for comfort and they are uncomfortable. You can be glad when that happens — give a cheer, even! — for though they don't like it, I do! And all heaven applauds. And know that you are in good company. My prophets and witnesses have always gotten into this kind of trouble.

Answer the following questions with an honest heart.

Share the answers that impact you the most with others in recovery.

What does amends mean? What is amends NOT? What are false motives for making amends?

_____
_____
_____
_____
_____
_____

What do you feel when someone is dodgy, suspicious, or indirect towards you?

_____
_____
_____
_____
_____
_____
_____

Name two positive changes you have seen in yourself since beginning recovery.

1. _____
_____
_____
_____

2. _____
_____
_____
_____

Name any examples of selfish motivation you've had when apologizing or making amends.

_____
_____
_____
_____
_____
_____

List any hopes you have about the outcome of making amends with those in your inventory.

_____
_____
_____
_____
_____
_____

List the self-care exercises you will need to practice while writing your amends. If you're not sure, reach out to others who've experienced the need for self-care while writing their amends.

_____
_____
_____
_____
_____
_____

What would it sound like to offer amends to yourself for the decisions you've made in your addictions? Consider adding yourself to your list of people to make amends to.

_____
_____
_____
_____
_____
_____

No matter what the outcome is for making amends, are you prepared? List possible outcomes you would need to be prepared for.

What behavior changes have you demonstrated that will serve as evidence of your current state of recovery?

How do you write an amends?

That question is rhetorical, but there is a great acronym for the structure for amends I heard from someone sharing their testimony about their amends. It is RUT - ABC. "When you're in a RUT, get out of it by following the ABC's."

R - Recognize the wrong

U - Understand the hurt

T - Take responsibility

A - Ask for forgiveness

BC – Behavior Change

Recognize the wrong: It is important that you start with and stay focused on your wrongs. This does not mean going into details about every specific instance of your wrongdoing. If the person brings up specific instances, which you have already acknowledged to yourself in inventory, then acknowledge that wrong to the person. Remember that it is not your job to control their emotions, and yes, they may experience a rollercoaster of emotions during the amends.

Understand the hurt: If the person interjects during this part of amends, give them the space to, and use that as an opportunity to understand their pain your wrong caused and is still causing for them.

R and U work together in amends. You may be going back and forth between the two. Give time and breathing room to the process of understanding the pain that your wrong caused them. So pause, breathe, and show them your sincerity, grief, and compassion. Give them eye contact here.

Take responsibility: Taking ownership of your wrong is a step towards being a healthy adult. We have been reacting and in our withholding behaviors for so long that we can often skip this step when forming intimacy by withholding, isolating, blaming, criticizing, and defending. It is crucial for the recipient to hear and feel a serious acknowledgement of responsibility.

Ask for forgiveness: This is what it says and nothing more. You are entering a vulnerable place where yes or no answers are both understandable. Prepare your heart for both. You should avoid pressuring the wounded person to forgive. This can be worded as a question or a statement.

Give pause after offering them a chance to forgive you.

Behavior Change: Speak to specific practices and habits you are practicing in your recovery. Express your praises on your road of recovery. Emphasize that you are still in process, taking things one day at a time, and will continue towards healing and recovery. This may also be a chance to stand under the wounded and their feelings from the amends. Asking them what they need from you – and then doing it, if it is a reasonable request from them – may be the next step for their healing.

In summary: this gives us a blueprint, like many of us need, to be able to structure amends. Realize that this is a process that healthy and recovered people make on a week-to-week/day-to-day basis when saying the wrong thing, getting defensive, or withholding intimacy.

Now, begin writing your amends for each person/group on your list. Use a separate document for each, or you may make it handwritten (especially if you plan to mail it or have it delivered).

Amends can be a step that takes a long time. That being said, it is important to begin planning out when, where, and how you will meet with those face-to-face amends recipients. In the amends tracker below, rewrite your list of people/groups, their location/number to contact, confirmation of amends offering being made, their response, and time/date/location of the planned amends.

Once you have an amends planned, it is important to rehearse and remind yourself of the reasons why you are giving amends. Who will you plan to rehearse with? Will you be open to feedback?

Remember not to give someone amends with the false expectation that they will reconcile with you. Their response to your amends is completely independent from the reasons why you are taking responsibility for your actions.

Amends Tracker/Planner/Reflection				
Person/ Organization	When	Location	Mode of Amends: Written/Letter Face-to-face Empty Chair	After Completed: My Feelings Their Reactions Outcome

Step 9 Summary

Congratulations on completing your ninth step.

- **Now, write a summary of what you have learned and experienced.**

    Include:

    - **Who were you able to deliver amends to? What was the outcome? Explain 1-2 of these experiences below.**
    - **How did God help you through this process of amends?**
    - **How did others in recovery help you through this process of amends?**

_____
_____
_____
_____
_____
_____
_____
_____
_____
_____
_____
_____
_____
_____
_____
_____
_____

Memory Verse:

2 Samuel 12: 13, 22-25 MSG
Then David confessed to Nathan, "I've sinned against God"... [then] David went and comforted his wife...

Prayer:

Father,

I know the terrible things I have done to myself, to others, and to my loved ones. I confess my sins against You. And like David, I confess my sins against my partner and loved ones. Give me the courage and grace to comfort my partner and my loved ones and to make amends with them.

Give me the grace to bear good fruit, the fruit of peace (Solomon) in all my relationships. Give me the grace to have affection for others, an exuberance for life, and serenity. Give me the grace to develop the willingness to stick with things, compassion of the heart, and a conviction that a basic holiness permeates all things and people. Give me the grace to be involved in loyal commitments, not needing to force my way in life but to be able to marshal and direct my energies wisely.

In Jesus' name, Amen.

Share your step summary with others in recovery. Be open to their feedback and what they have found in the importance of Step 9.

STEP 10

Step 10 - We continue to take personal inventory and, when in the wrong, we promptly admit it.

Memory Verse:

James 5:16 MSG "Make this your common practice: Confess your sins to each other and pray for each other so that you can live together whole and healed. The prayer of a person living right with God is something powerful to be reckoned with."

Goals

- From this point on, the end of this process is only the beginning.
  - The purpose of the 12 steps is to give you a new way to live your life. The primary way we do this in recovery is to have an open, honest, and ongoing personal inventory.
- Honesty is the goal, the main goal, the only goal in this step.

Proverbs 11:16 MSG
The integrity of the honest keeps them on track; the deviousness of crooks brings them to ruin.

Expectations

- **Your routines will begin to change.**
  - Daily recovery work will begin evolving into fewer questions to answer in the step work and more reflection about everyday living.

- Immediately admitting you're wrong should be something you are practicing regularly already with weekly check-ins.
- Honesty becomes a way of living now, and going back to secrecy needs to be a thing of the past.

Proverbs 19: 8, 9 MSG
Grow a wise heart—you'll do yourself a favor; keep a clear head—you'll find a good life. The person who tells lies gets caught; the person who spreads rumors is ruined.

Hurdles

- Temptation will always be present in your life of recovery.
  - The truth is that we all slip and are not perfect.
  - Secrecy will be a temptation that can set you back, returning to steps 1, 2, and 3.
- Remember the cost and destruction from your withholding behaviors.
- This step is the launching point into lifelong healing and recovery. When the 12 steps are over, the fight isn't.
- You are worth a life of authentic relationships and freedom from your withholding behaviors.

Proverbs 6:16-23 MSG
Here are six things God hates, and one more that He loathes with a passion: eyes that are arrogant, a tongue that lies, hands that murder the innocent, a heart that hatches evil plots, feet that race down a wicked track, a mouth that lies under oath, a troublemaker in the family.

Good friend, follow your father's good advice; don't wander off from your mother's teachings. Wrap yourself in them from head to foot; wear them like a scarf around your neck. Wherever you walk, they'll guide you; whenever you rest, they'll guard you; when you wake up, they'll tell you what's next. For sound advice is a beacon, good teaching is a light, moral discipline is a life path.

Answer the following questions with an honest heart.

Share the answers that impact you the most with others in recovery.

You might want to photocopy the questions below so you can use them daily or weekly for ongoing 10th Step inventory work.

Have you felt fear, anxiety, anger, defensiveness, or the desire to control this week? If so, do you know what's happening in your life that is at the heart of those emotions?

_____
_____
_____
_____
_____
_____
_____
_____

Have your character defects been evident to you or others today? And if so, how?

_____
_____
_____
_____
_____
_____
_____
_____

Have any of your recent actions required amends or correction in the past week? And if so, how?

_____
_____
_____
_____
_____
_____
_____

Name an action you can take today to give yourself forgiveness and love in acceptance of your imperfections. Share this with someone in recovery who has completed their Step 10 and write down an action they've taken.

_____
_____
_____
_____
_____
_____
_____

Step 10 is a practice. Acceptance of yourself, self-care, and self-forgiveness are a practice. Plan a time and space each day in which you can practice Step 10.

_____
_____
_____
_____
_____
_____
_____

Write or copy down a prayer you will use during your daily time to practice Step 10.

_____
_____
_____
_____
_____
_____

How have you asked for help and received it today?

_____
_____
_____
_____
_____
_____
_____
_____
_____
_____
_____

What opportunities have you had today to help others?

_____
_____
_____
_____
_____
_____
_____
_____
_____
_____

Journaling exercise:

Over the next 2 weeks of your recovery, create a daily inventory of the issues and struggles that brought you to recovery, including but not exclusive to:

Dishonesty, Fear, Pride, Control, Defensiveness, Greed, Criticism, Blame, Impulsiveness, Impatience, Self-Critical, Perfectionism, Sarcasm, Manipulation

Refer back to your Step 4 to remind yourself of what a daily inventory should look like.

Week One/Day One

_____
_____
_____
_____
_____
_____
_____
_____
_____
_____

Week One/Day Two

_____
_____
_____
_____
_____
_____
_____
_____
_____

Week One/Day Three

Week One/Day Four

Week One/Day Five

THE 12 STEPS TO BECOMING WELL

Week One/Day Six

Week One/Day Seven

Week Two/Day One

Week Two/Day Two

Week Two/Day Three

Week Two/Day Four

Week Two/Day Five

Week Two/Day Six

Week Two/Day Seven

Did you admit struggles/behaviors in your daily inventory? How do you plan to make amends for these daily inventories?

_____
_____
_____
_____
_____
_____
_____

What tools do you have that will help you recognize your daily inventory?

_____
_____
_____
_____
_____
_____
_____

When do you schedule your daily inventory? Why does this time work best for you?

_____
_____
_____
_____
_____
_____

When will you be able to have an inventory check-in with your recovery partner?

_____
_____
_____
_____
_____
_____
_____

How will making a daily inventory aid your growth in recovery?

_____
_____
_____
_____
_____
_____
_____

Why is it important to admit your wrongs quickly? Who benefits from this step in your recovery and why?

_____
_____
_____
_____
_____
_____
_____

Explain the last time you were caught off guard by an addiction that you thought was under control.

_____
_____
_____
_____
_____
_____
_____

Describe the encouragement and/or discouragement you feel about your recovery needing daily practices.

_____
_____
_____
_____
_____
_____
_____

Identify a weakness you have found strength from by relying upon God. Then identify a weakness you are still trying to overcome by your own strength.

_____
_____
_____
_____
_____

Name the thoughts that tempt you regularly.

In what ways, if any, are fear, guilt, or shame still affecting your ability to completely give or receive love? Write Proverbs 6:16-23 here and insert your name in it.

What areas of your life do you still need to surrender and hand over to God?

List any fears, resentments, or pains affecting how you are responding to others. How are you responding to God?

_____
_____
_____
_____
_____
_____
_____

Identify any areas of your life for which you doubt God's will over your own.

_____
_____
_____
_____
_____
_____
_____

List any desires you have that overshadow consideration of others or wise counsel from others.

_____
_____
_____
_____
_____
_____
_____

Are there any hurts or traumas you still need to grieve? If so, please list them. Consider sharing them with a recovery partner and seeking advice for how to grieve properly.

_____
_____
_____
_____
_____
_____
_____
_____
_____
_____

Are you needing to change any daily choices, behaviors, or habits that lead you to slip? List these changes and share them with a recovery partner. Give updates to your accountability partner and during weekly group.

_____
_____
_____
_____
_____
_____
_____
_____
_____
_____

Step 10 Summary

Congratulations on completing your tenth step.

- **Now, write a summary of what you have learned and experienced.**

Include:

- **Any ongoing struggles/behaviors you are creating inventories for.**
- **Your top 3 self-care exercises that help you in continuing recovery, with reasons why for each.**

_____
_____
_____
_____
_____
_____
_____
_____
_____
_____
_____
_____
_____
_____
_____
_____
_____
_____
_____
_____

THE 12 STEPS TO BECOMING WELL

Memory Verse:

James 5:16 MSG
Make this your common practice: Confess your sins to each other and pray for each other so that you can live together whole and healed. The prayer of a person living right with God is something powerful to be reckoned with.

Prayer:

Father,

I will make this my common practice. I will confess my sins to a trusted Christian and we will pray for each other so I can live freely without shame with my family and within my Christian community. This will make me whole in my spirit, soul, and body, and wholeness brings healing to me. My prayer is powerful because I am living right before God and man.

My prayers are answered in Jesus' name, Amen!

Share your step summary with others in recovery. Be open to their feedback and what they have found in the importance of Step 10.

BECOMING WELL
STEP 11

Step 11 - We seek to improve contact with God through prayer and meditation, praying for knowledge of His will for our lives and the power to carry it out.

Memory Verse:

Matthew 6:9-13 NIV "Our Father in heaven, hallowed be your name, your kingdom come, your will be done, on earth as it is in heaven. Give us today our daily bread. And forgive us our debts, as we also have forgiven our debtors. And lead us not into temptation, but deliver us from the evil one."

Goals

- We started with relying upon God, and we end with relying upon God.
- Creating ongoing habits, devotionals and, meditations will center your life on a will greater than your own
- Continue to build upon your current relationship with God
- Claim a life of peace with God as your provider, not people, not materials, not your past coping mechanisms.

Romans 12:1, 2 AMP
Therefore I urge you, brothers and sisters, by the mercies of God, to present your bodies [dedicating all of yourselves, set apart] as a living sacrifice, holy and well-pleasing to God, which is your rational (logical, intelligent) act of worship.

And do not be conformed to this world [any longer with its superficial values and customs], but be transformed and progressively changed [as you mature spiritually] by the renewing of your mind [focusing on godly values and ethical attitudes], so that you may prove [for yourselves] what the will of God is, that which is good and acceptable and perfect [in His plan and purpose for you].

Expectations

- Your spiritual walk is only as good as how much effort you put into it.
  - This is your daily choice to put God or idols first in your heart
- Surrendering your own will and seeking God's will for your life is a practice, not a faucet or light switch
- Whether in good times or desperate ones, you will continue to need to seek God in order to seek ongoing recovery

1 Peter 1: 13-16 AMP
So prepare your minds for action, be completely sober [in spirit—steadfast, self-disciplined, spiritually and morally alert], fix your hope completely on the grace [of God] that is coming to you when Jesus Christ is revealed. 14 [Live] as obedient children [of God]; do not be conformed to the evil desires which governed you in your ignorance [before you knew the requirements and transforming power of the good news regarding salvation]. 15 But like the Holy One who called you, be holy yourselves in all your conduct [be set apart from the world by your godly character and moral courage]; 16 because it is written, "YOU SHALL BE HOLY (set apart), FOR I AM HOLY."

Hurdles

- Feelings are not always something to be followed
  - Our own will gets in the way sometimes
  - Thinking you got it under control will lead to arrogance and pride
  - Boasting will lead to self-centeredness
- Remember how God has helped you in this walk of recovery. He will be what leads you into a life of walking in humility and peace.

Jeremiah 17:9, 10 MSG
"The heart is hopelessly dark and deceitful, a puzzle that no one can figure out.
But I, God, search the heart and examine the mind. I get to the heart of the human.
I get to the root of things. I treat them as they really are, not as they pretend to be."

1 Corinthians 2:16 AMP
For who has known or understood the mind (the counsels and purposes) of the Lord so as to guide and instruct Him and give Him knowledge? But we have the mind of Christ (the Messiah) and do hold the thoughts (feelings and purposes) of His heart.

FROM INTIMACY AVOIDANCE FOR CHRISTIANS

Answer the following questions with an honest heart.

Share the answers that impact you the most with others in recovery.

List the things that you are grateful for.

_____
_____
_____
_____
_____
_____
_____
_____
_____
_____
_____

What do your prayer and meditation practices currently look like?

_____
_____
_____
_____
_____
_____
_____
_____
_____
_____
_____

Share your prayer and meditation practices with someone in recovery. Reflect with them on ways to improve or polish the practice to be more intimate with God. Record details of that conversation here and come up with an action plan.

_____
_____
_____
_____
_____
_____
_____

Are there any ways you have begun trying to take your will and control back from God?

_____
_____
_____
_____
_____
_____
_____

How will you begin surrendering your will back over to God in these areas?

_____
_____
_____
_____
_____
_____
_____

How do you define prayer? How does God define prayer?

_____
_____
_____
_____
_____
_____
_____

List out the overall benefits to your mental, physical, and relational health from daily prayer habits.

_____
_____
_____
_____
_____
_____
_____

How do you define meditation? How does God define meditation?

_____
_____
_____
_____
_____
_____

Do you harbor anger toward God that results in avoidance of prayer and meditation? If so, reach out to others in recovery to help resolve your anger.

_____
_____
_____
_____
_____
_____

What issues do you have relaxing due to other coping mechanisms you use? Including but not limited to caffeine, nicotine, adrenaline, or sugar.

_____
_____
_____
_____
_____
_____

Was there a time in your past when you misunderstood God's will for you? If so, record those misunderstandings.

_____
_____
_____
_____
_____
_____

What is the difference in how you now see God's will for your life, as opposed to prior to entering recovery?

_____
_____
_____
_____
_____
_____

Describe the importance of following God's will for your life.

_____
_____
_____
_____
_____
_____
_____

How has God helped you carry out His will for your life?

_____
_____
_____
_____
_____
_____

Create a future action plan for your prayer life. Note the best time, place, and reason for the necessity of daily prayer. Identify how you can practice prayer and meditation throughout the day.

_____
_____
_____
_____
_____
_____
_____
_____

Journaling your prayer and meditation time and contact with God is meant to grow you spiritually.

Spend 3 days recording the prayers you make on a day-to-day basis. If it becomes something you would like to commit to on a long-term basis, do so.

Day One

_____
_____
_____
_____
_____
_____
_____
_____
_____

Day Two

Day Three

Step 11 Summary

Congratulations on completing your eleventh step.

- **Now, write a summary of what you have learned about yourself in the space below. Include:**

  - **What you have learned about yourself, your withholding behaviors, and what you must choose to do in order to stay in recovery.**
  - **A summary of your future action plan for continuing prayer and meditation**

_____
_____
_____
_____
_____
_____
_____
_____
_____
_____
_____
_____
_____
_____
_____
_____
_____
_____
_____
_____

Memory Verse:

Matthew 6:9-13 NIV
"Our Father in heaven, hallowed be your name, your kingdom come, your will be done, on earth as it is in heaven. Give us today our daily bread. And forgive us our debts, as we also have forgiven our debtors. And lead us not into temptation, but deliver us from the evil one."

Prayer:

My Father in heaven,

Hallowed be Your name. Your kingdom comes. Your will be done for my life here on earth as it is in heaven. Give me this day my daily bread. Forgive me my debts as I have forgiven my debtors. Lead me not into temptation but deliver me from the evil one.

In Jesus' name, Amen.

Share your step summary with others in recovery. Be open to their feedback and what they have found in the importance of Step 11.

STEP 12

Step 12 - Having had a spiritual awakening from our experience through the steps, we seek to share with others and practice our principles in all our relationships.

Memory Verse:

Colossians 3:12, 13 MSG "So, chosen by God for this new life of love, dress in the wardrobe God picked out for you: compassion, kindness, humility, quiet strength, discipline. Be even-tempered, content with second place, quick to forgive an offense. Forgive as quickly and completely as the Master forgave you."

Goals

- Pray for God to use you, and to open doors to what may come next in your walk of recovery.
- Assess the season you're in.
- Stay connected with others in recovery even after commencing.
- Commencement means you aren't finished yet and will always be in the process.

Colossians 3: 14, 15 MSG
And regardless of what else you put on, wear love. It's your basic, all-purpose garment. Never be without it. Let the peace of Christ keep you in tune with each other, in step with each other. None of this going off and doing your own thing. And cultivate thankfulness. Let the Word of Christ—the Message—have the run of the house. Give it plenty of room in your lives.

Expectations

- **You can develop purpose for your life in recovery.**
  - **God can use you and your story to impact the lives of others if you allow it.**
  - **Relationships with those seeking a better, freer life from struggles will be unlike others, more vulnerable and loving**
- **Behaviors that you keep and take with you will be the evidence of real change**

Colossians 3: 16, 17 MSG
Instruct and direct one another using good common sense. And sing, sing your hearts out to God! Let every detail in your lives—words, actions, whatever—be done in the name of the Master, Jesus, thanking God the Father every step of the way.

Hurdles

- **Closing yourself off to God or His purposes can feel tempting**
  - **Keeping your story to yourself**
  - **Thinking you got this now on your own**
  - **Resorting to old habits out of resentment from lost relationships**
- **Remember that God wants a new life for you. You are worth lifelong healing and recovery.**
- **With the progress you've made, practice gratitude, and use any exercise up until this point whenever you need.**
- **Keep going, keep relying, keep believing that you are worth it!**

Colossians 3: 22-25 MSG
And don't just do the minimum that will get you by. Do your best. Work from the heart for your real Master, for God, confident that you'll get paid in full when you come into your inheritance. Keep in mind always that the ultimate Master you're serving is Christ. The sullen servant who does shoddy work will be held responsible. Being a follower of Jesus doesn't cover up bad work.

Answer the following questions with an honest heart.

Share the answers that impact you the most with others in recovery.

How does serving others benefit my recovery?

_____
_____
_____
_____
_____
_____
_____

In what ways can I serve my recovery group?

_____
_____
_____
_____
_____
_____
_____

Are my motives to help and serve others selfless and expecting nothing in return? What are my reasons when I help and serve others?

_____
_____
_____
_____
_____
_____
_____

THE 12 STEPS TO BECOMING WELL

How will selflessly serving others progress my own recovery?

_____
_____
_____
_____
_____
_____
_____

Create a plan, using your answers from above, for how you will serve others in and out of recovery after you are done with your 12th step. Include loved ones, family, friends, coworkers, employees, and the recovery group.	
Person/Group/ Organization	**Plan to Serve them by…**

How are you spiritually different since entering recovery? Describe the difference in terms of your beliefs and feelings.

_____
_____
_____
_____
_____
_____
_____

What is your current emotional state now that you are completing Step 12, and why?

_____
_____
_____
_____
_____
_____
_____

What would you say to encourage others who are still struggling in their recovery?

_____
_____
_____
_____
_____
_____

THE 12 STEPS TO BECOMING WELL

How will you plan to practice the twelve steps in your day-to-day life?

_____
_____
_____
_____
_____
_____
_____

Name specific ways your behavior has been an example of your recovery. At work? At home? With family?

_____
_____
_____
_____
_____
_____
_____

What service opportunities in your area, life, church, or career do you feel passionate about?

_____
_____
_____
_____
_____
_____

What steps were most influential in your recovery and why?

What is most important to you as you end the 12-step process?

Step 12 Summary

Congratulations on completing your twelfth step.

- Now, write a summary of what you have learned about yourself in the space below. Include:

  - **Encouragement toward other participants for the full completion of the twelve steps.**
  - **A summary of your action plan to serve others (in any area of your life).**

- **Describe why two of the steps (your choice) were most influential to you.**
- **Write out Colossians 3:12-25 and insert your name in these verses.**

_____
_____
_____
_____
_____
_____
_____
_____
_____
_____
_____
_____
_____
_____
_____
_____
_____
_____

Memory Verse:

Colossians 3:12, 13 MSG
So, chosen by God for this new life of love, dress in the wardrobe God picked out for you: compassion, kindness, humility, quiet strength, discipline. Be even-tempered, content with second place, quick to forgive an offense. Forgive as quickly and completely as the Master forgave you.

Prayer:

Father,

I am chosen by You. You have chosen me to live a new life of love. I will dress in the wardrobe that You picked out for me. I will dress in compassion, kindness, humility, quiet strength, and discipline. I will be even-tempered, content with second place, quick to forgive an offense. I will forgive as quickly and completely as the Master forgave me. I will always wear a garment of love. It's my basic, all-purpose garment. I will never be without it. I will let the peace of Christ keep me in tune with others, in step with others. None of this going off and doing my own thing. I cultivate thankfulness. I let the Word of Christ—the Message—have the run of my house. I give it plenty of room in my life. I will instruct and direct others using good common sense. And I will sing, sing my heart out to God! I will let every detail in my life—words, actions, whatever—be done in the name of the Master, Jesus, thanking God the Father every step of the way.

And I won't just do the minimum that will get me by. I will do my best. Work from the heart for my real Master, for God, confident that I'll get paid in full when I come into my inheritance. I will always keep in mind that the ultimate Master I'm serving is Christ. I will never be the sullen servant who does shoddy work and be held responsible. Being a follower of Jesus doesn't cover up bad work. I will be all that I can be for Christ! He gave His all for me and I will give my all to Him!

In Jesus' name, Amen.

Share your step summary with others in recovery. Be open to their feedback and what they have found in the importance of Step 12.

Parting Words

In closing, I would like to thank you for reading this book. We hope that it was helpful to you. While I know the road is long and tough to navigate, I encourage you to keep pressing on. As Winston Churchill once said, *"If you are going through hell, keep going."* If you do the work, don't give in, and seek help along the way, I know you will find your way out of the painful circumstances in which you have found yourself. We wish you healing, comfort, peace, and wholeness in your recovery journey.

Addendum

Feeling Wheel

The Twelve Steps for Intimacy Avoidance

1. We admitted we were powerless over our intimacy avoidance and that our lives had become unmanageable.

2. We came to believe that a power greater than ourselves could restore us to sanity.

3. We made a decision to turn our will and lives over to the care of God as we understand Him.

4. We made a searching and fearless moral inventory of ourselves.

5. We admitted to God, to ourselves, and to others the exact nature of our wrongs.

6. We were entirely ready to have God remove all these defects of character.

7. We humbly asked God to remove our struggle.

8. We made a list of all people we had harmed, and we became willing to make amends with them all.

9. We made direct amends to whomever possible, except when to do so would injure them or others.

10. We continue to take personal inventory and, when in the wrong, we promptly admit it.

11. We seek through prayer and meditation to improve contact with God, praying for knowledge of His will for our lives and the strength to carry it out.

12. Having had a spiritual awakening from our experience through the steps, we seek to share with others and practice our principles in all our relationships.

The Twelve Steps of AA (Alcoholics Anonymous)

1. We admitted we were powerless over alcohol — that our lives had become unmanageable.

2. Came to believe that a power greater than ourselves could restore us to sanity.

3. Made a decision to turn our will and our lives over to the care of our God as we understand Him.

4. Made a searching and fearless moral inventory of ourselves.

5. Admitted to God, to ourselves, and to another human being the exact nature of our wrongs.

6. Were entirely ready to have God remove all these defects of character.

7. Humbly asked God to remove our shortcomings.

8. Made a list of all persons we had harmed, and became willing to make amends to them all.

9. Made direct amends to such people wherever possible, except when to do so would injure them or others.

10. Continued to take personal inventory and when we were wrong promptly admitted it.

11. Sought through prayer and meditation to improve our conscious contact with God as we understood Him, praying only for knowledge of His will for us and the power to carry that out.

12. Having had a spiritual awakening as the result of these Steps, we tried to carry this message to alcoholics, and to practice these principles in all our affairs.

Recovery and 12 Step Prayers

Third Step Prayer (Page 63, AA Big Book)

God, I offer myself to Thee — to build with me and to do with me as Thou wilt. Relieve me of the bondage of self, that I may better do Thy will. Take away my difficulties, that victory over them may bear witness to those I would help of Thy Power, Thy Love, and Thy Way of life. May I do Thy will always!

Fourth Step Prayer (Page 67, AA Big Book)

This is a sick man. How can I be helpful to him? God, save me from being angry. Thy will be done.

Seventh Step Prayer (Page 76, AA Big Book)

My Creator, I am now willing that you should have all of me, good & bad. I pray that you now remove from me every single defect of character that stands in the way of my usefulness to you & my fellows. Grant me strength, as I go from here to do Your bidding. Amen.

Eighth Step Prayer (Page 76, AA Big Book)

Faith without works is dead.

Tenth Step Prayer (Page 85, AA Big Book)

How can I serve Thee? Thy will (not mine) be done.

Eleventh Step Prayer (Twelve Steps and Twelve Traditions, p. 99)

Lord, make me a channel of Thy peace – that where there is hatred, I may bring love – that where there is wrong, I may bring the spirit of forgiveness – that where there is discord, I may bring harmony – that where there is error, I may bring truth--that where there is doubt, I may bring faith--that where there is despair, I may bring hope – that where there are shadows, I may bring light – that where there is sadness, I may bring joy. Lord, grant that I may seek to comfort rather than to be comforted – to understand, than to be understood – to love, than to be loved. For it is by self-forgetting that one finds. It is by forgiving that one is forgiven. It is by dying that one awakens to eternal life. Amen

Serenity Prayer (Reinhold Niebuhr)

God, grant me the serenity to accept the things I cannot change,
The courage to change the things I can,
And the wisdom to know the difference.

40 ways to be IA (Intimacy Avoidant)

1. Marked lack of empathy. Has trouble putting themselves in someone else's shoes. Often comes off as insensitive or uncaring. When others try to share their perspective, they often impose their own views on the situation without listening to the other person's view. Often has trouble understanding cause and effect - in other words, how their actions are contributing to the reactions of others.

2. Oversensitivity to criticism or perceives criticism when there is none. This may stem from a fear of rejection, poor self-esteem, or a generally negative view of others' intentions. Oversensitivity to criticism has been linked to negative childhood experiences such as harsh criticism from a parent or caregiver, rejection from peers, or having a parent with unrealistically high expectations. People who are oversensitive to criticism (real or perceived) often have negative cognitive biases that cause them to interpret information in a negative way.

3. Low emotional expression and bandwidth. Has an inability or unwillingness (oftentimes both) to express emotion. Emotional range is generally very small (2 or 3 emotions shared, usually some type of anger). The term "emotional bandwidth" refers to someone's ability to handle or engage in emotional stimuli, whether the stimulus is their own or someone else's.

4. Jumps to conclusions. Involves jumping to conclusions without having supporting facts. Mind-reading is when people randomly conclude that others are reacting negatively to them. Fortune-telling is assuming things are going to turn out badly and acting like those assumptions are already established facts.

5. Contempt for self/others. Contempt for self often comes across as shame and/or self-pity. Contempt for others comes out as grandiosity, belittling, or criticism.

6. Sabotages emotional connectedness. According to research studies, people who sabotage their relationships often have low self-esteem, difficulty trusting people (especially their partners), and a fear of commitment or being hurt, abandoned, or rejected.

7. Reactive vs. Proactive in relationships. This person appears ambivalent or disinterested in creating opportunities for ongoing, consistent connectedness. Major efforts to show love to their partner only come when the partner is fed up and entertaining the thought of ending the relationship. These efforts often fade away once the partner is reconnected to them, leading to an ongoing cycle that alternates between disinterest, emotional pain, and love-bombing.

8. Spiritually independent or disengaged. This person refuses to share any intimate details of their spirituality with their partner, often claiming that their spirituality is "private".

9. Requires Hoop Jumping. Often a feature of Intimacy Avoidant relationships, the IA will make their partner jump through a series of "hoops" to receive love. Much of this behavior is born out of entitlement. IAs often use this behavior as an excuse to withhold intimacy from their partner or criticize them for a "lack of performance."

10. Defensiveness. Defensive people often have issues of power and control. They often perceive confrontation and/or accountability as threats. The purpose of defensiveness is typically to protect a person from feeling hurt or shame. Defensiveness comes in many forms, including blame-shifting, silence, denial, and even self-pity.

11. Prideful and/or Unteachable. Typically, a person is masking feelings of low self-esteem and self-worth with pride. Pride is often a byproduct of feelings of inadequacy and vulnerability. Being "unteachable" can stem from pride, jealousy, stress, anxiety, or feelings of inadequacy.

12. Blame-shifting. People who blame-shift are often in denial about their level of personal responsibility. They often can't accept the fact that they may be at least partially responsible for a failure or mistake. Another reason for blame-shifting is to make the other person feel guilty or shamed, to silence them.

13. Offends from the victim position. This takes place when a person decides that their role as victim gives them the right to lash out and/or hurt others. Pia Mellody and Terrence Real call this "retaliation." Intimacy Avoidant people often put themselves in the victim position through blame-shifting, shame, and self-pity. This makes it easier to justify bad behavior.

14. Suspicious of partner. There are many reasons IAs are suspicious of their partners. Common reasons include adverse childhood experiences that cause a general lack of trust toward others, depression and anxiety, and negative experiences in past relationships.

15. Gaslighting. Gaslighting is defined as psychological manipulation, typically over a prolonged period, that causes the victim to question their thoughts, feelings, memories, and perception of reality. Gaslighting typically involves lying but is not the same as lying. People often lie to escape consequences. Gaslighters lie to intentionally cause someone else to doubt themselves.

16. Stonewalling/Punishing through anger. Uses anger or silence to control the conversation. With silence, the partner eventually gives up, which is the intent. Anger is often used to intimidate, and punishing through anger is done purposely to teach the person a lesson and make them think twice about saying anything again. In either case, both are being used to silence someone.

17. Frequent lying. For IAs, lying often comes in the form of leaving out important information to avoid unwanted consequences. In some cases, habitual lying can be a sign of a more serious personality disorder.

18. Avoids taking responsibility for actions. This can be a result of emotional immaturity, denial, a refusal to be vulnerable, or an avoidance of intense feelings of remorse, guilt, and/or shame. In more serious cases, it can be because the person truly feels that accepting consequences is beneath them or does not have any understanding that their actions have consequences.

19. Breadcrumbing or Love Bombing. Breadcrumbing is a form of manipulation in which a person gives another person just enough attention and/or love to string them along. Love bombing often comes in the form of excessive flattery, attention, or gifts being used to lure someone to gain security for themselves.

20. Emotionally disengaged. This often stems from a deep fear of being ridiculed or rejected. An emotionally disengaged person may have learned from previous relationships that showing emotions made them vulnerable to negative consequences. Emotional disengagement is often developed in the family of origin when one or both parents failed to communicate their emotions or were uncomfortable with the emotions of others.

21. Feelings are facts. A person who treats feelings as facts often experiences emotions so intensely that they feel real. This typically stems from emotional immaturity. It's related to the cognitive distortion of emotional reasoning: "I feel it, so it must be true."

22. Poor self reflection. Otherwise known as a lack of self-awareness. People with poor self-reflection are often intensely afraid of judgement and rejection from others. They keep themselves in a "protective bubble." This "bubble" makes it difficult for them to get in touch with their inner selves.

23. Self-preoccupation. This often stems from early childhood experiences of feeling rejected by others. They also could have been brought up to believe that they didn't have to consider the feelings of others. Trauma can also play a role because the person may have learned that they couldn't trust others, and this developed into self-preoccupation. Self-preoccupied people are generally emotionally immature.

24. Labels themselves and others. Related to the cognitive distortion of Labeling, which is a form of overgeneralization. It can also be related to perfectionism. For example, instead of being able to accept that they made a mistake, a person might label themselves a "loser." Instead of being understanding about the faults of others, they may label others "losers" or "idiots." Instead of describing a situation realistically, labeling typically involves using inflammatory terms and language.

25. Focuses on the faults of others. Typically used as a defense mechanism in order to avoid feelings of guilt, shame, or inadequacy. It can also stem from entitlement when a person feels everyone else it at fault for them not getting what they want or feel they deserve.

26. Objectification. Treats their partner, others, and even themselves as objects. This extends far past sexual objectification or reducing someone to the sum of their body parts. Objectification also shows up as treating someone as if there is no need to be concerned about their experiences and/or feelings, a refusal to honor boundaries, treating people as if they were tools to be used for the IA to achieve their own goals, and treating someone as if they were easily replaced with someone else (a refusal to acknowledge someone's uniqueness).

27. Poor demeanor. Acts frequently disgruntled, angry, or irritated. Doesn't listen to their partner's feelings or discounts their experience. When asked to participate in the nurturing of the relationship, acts like it's a huge imposition. When asked to be accountable for past and/or present actions, responds with anger, blame, or pouting.

28. Sexually disconnected or avoidant. Doesn't make eye contact during sex or is mentally "checked out." Sex often feels empty and transactional to the partner. Also common is a complete/almost complete avoidance of sex. Couples that have sex 6 or fewer times per year are considered to have a "sexless" relationship.

29. Sexual gratification outside of committed relationship. This isn't always the case, but when it is it's typically due to an inability to connect with the partner. For most, this will be done through pornography and masturbation. For some, it will involve getting emotionally or sexually connected with a real person who is not their partner. Sexual addiction and attachment disorders are often underlying issues, especially with serial cheating.

30. Inability to handle conflict productively. For some, this will show up as conflict avoidance, stonewalling, and/or people-pleasing. For others, this will involve blame-shifting, denial, and overall defensiveness.

31. All-or-nothing thinking (black-and-white thinking). Seeing things in black and white without shades of gray. Tends to associate others and self into 2 categories: good and bad. Signs of all-or-nothing thinking include a tendency to use extreme terms when describing things, perfectionism, inability to see both good and bad in people and/or self, negative self-talk, and fear of trying new things.

32. An intense need to be right. Possible reasons for always needing to be right include insecurity, a need for control, a fear of failure, a competitive nature, and cognitive biases or distortions (such as all-or-nothing thinking) that make it difficult to consider alternate perspectives or admit it when wrong.

33. Easily offended. Often related to the cognitive distortion of personalization, which is assigning blame to oneself for circumstances out of one's control. Other reasons include unresolved psychological or emotional issues, a perception that their honor or personally held beliefs are being attacked, a generally negative emotional state, or the struggle to consider another's point of view.

34. Maximization and minimization of faults and/or good deeds. Tends to see others' faults as "huge" and their own as "not so bad." Tends to see their contributions as "huge" and others' contributions as minimal. In extreme cases, this can be due to grandiosity that contributes to a false sense of self-importance.

35. Constant activity that disrupts relational connection. Many workaholics seek approval and become overly focused on work and "busyness" to gain approval and respect from others. Sometimes workaholism also occurs when the person is trying to avoid intimacy in their relationships.

36. Plays the victim. Playing the victim is a manipulative tactic. It is often used to avoid taking responsibility, gain sympathy and attention from others, and/or to discredit the experience and feelings of a person they have wronged.

37. Hero or Zero. Since IAs tend to see things in black and white without shades of gray, they tend to see themselves as a complete "hero" without faults or a "zero" with nothing but faults. This mentality often leads to blame-shifting, going "victim," and even complete denial of the issues.

38. I did it my way. This is an unwillingness to accept influence from their partner. IAs are typically highly independent and often don't listen to the suggestions of their partners when making decisions. Many partners define an IA partner as "an island."

39. Cynical Script. A bad story being played repeatedly in the person's head to excuse their poor treatment of the partner. The cynical script is often used to play the victim.

40. Married but Unloved: If married, the partner feels as if they are alone in it all. Many partners married to Intimacy Avoidants describe this as a surprise. It is common for Intimacy Avoidants to act differently before marriage than after marriage. Once the commitment to marriage is made, Intimacy Avoidants start to pull away from their partners in the ways that matter most. Partners may describe the relationship as sexless, devoid of intimacy, and disconnected.

Resources

Men's Becoming Well Workgroups

Some guys have been in groups before; others have not. If you're committed to recovery from Sexual Addiction, Intimacy Avoidance, or Infidelity and are committed to rebuilding trust in your marriage, then our Men's Becoming Well Workgroups will be a good fit for you. Our men's groups focus on building and maintaining integrity, restoring intimacy in relationships, and rebuilding trust. They concentrate on two things: how to stop acting out and be accountable for the behavior that is breaking trust in the relationship, and how to develop the character and empathy it will take to support the relationship moving forward. And unlike many recovery groups out there, our guys are both finding sobriety and maintaining it.

Our groups are led by trained facilitators who have walked through many of these issues themselves, know how to stay sober, and know how to win in their relationship. The groups are small in size (no more than 8 people) so that each person can get the attention they need to address specific issues.

Each week, participants will hear teaching from a trained professional and receive assignments and exercises that facilitate recovery for both themselves and their relationships. Participants will also have access to an online education portal, videos that explain the concepts talked about during group, and tutorials on how to work exercises and complete assignments.

Another thing that makes our groups different is that we welcome input from the wounded partners. Most programs exclude the partner, expecting that they stay in a relationship and take their partner's word for it that they're doing the work. When we hear from partners about past experiences, they often complain that nothing was shared with them, and they didn't even know what was going on most of the time.

Although we want to stress that the men need to own and work through their own recovery, and no partner can do that for them, we assign exercises to include the partner in rebuilding the relationship. Additionally, we offer a free monthly video conference call in which we update partners on what the guys will be working on that month and allow them to ask questions. Those meetings are typically led by Matt and Laura Burton personally.

Join a Men's Becoming Well workgroup today
www.MyBecomingWell.com

Guys Group Intensives

Aka Men's Becoming Well Bootcamps

Are you a guy or married to a guy who's stuck or in a downward spiral, relationally or in your individual recovery, unable to do what's needed/necessary to heal the shattered trust in your relationship?

Our Guys Group Intensives focus on moving guys from playing to not lose to playing to win. Moving from working your relational and individual recovery as a way to avoid losing the relationship to doing it to win - win your partner's heart and trust back, and win back your life and your integrity.

These unique intensives are 3 days long and address issues related to intimacy avoidance, sexual or pornography addiction, and infidelity. Bootcamps are limited to 12 participants at a time.

These intensives are especially helpful to anyone whose partner is not ready to participate in a recovery program, guys who are stuck, or guys new to recovery who want to get off to a great start. Participants have the added bonus of getting to know other men who can provide support and accountability throughout the recovery process.

This is great option for anyone wanting to accelerate the healing process, because intensives take 4-6 months' worth of session work and condense it into 3 days. You will receive an assessment of your unique issues, 7-8 hours per day of instruction, exercises and tools to help you move forward, and a personalized recovery plan for yourself and/or your relationship. We provide you a shame-free environment to address your specific issues.

We need you to learn how to stand "Shoulder to Shoulder with your partner in their pain." We spend a lot of time in the Guys Group Intensives showing you, teaching you, and having you practice how to do that. It makes many times the difference along with embracing your own recovery on whether the relationship is able to find long-term healing and be saved.

Our intensive center in located in beautiful, sunny Tucson, Arizona.

Learn more or sign up for a Guys Group Intensive today

www.MyBecomingWell.com

Private Couple's Intensive

Moving couples from "Shattered to Strong"

Couples that attend Our One-on-One Private Couple's Intensives say it helps couples understand and begin or advance the long journey of healing from the immediate and ongoing impacts of porn addiction, sexual addiction, infidelity &/or Intimacy avoidance - for both the Wounding and Wounded partner. We are able to take the time to deep-dive into what's specifically destroying the trust, individually and as a couple, and find the recovery you're desperately trying to either rediscover or discover for the first time.

For many couples, this intensive is their last stop before divorce court or a decision to stay permanent roommates. Couple after couple says that their time at the intensive allowed them to identify and begin the process of healing the hurt and devastation, as well as giving them a new relational system, as their current one just doesn't work for many reasons.

If you choose a Private Couple's Intensive, we will work with you to identify your specific needs to make sure your concerns are fully addressed in a private setting. Our Private Couple's Intensives are 3 days in length and will address both people in the relationship individually as well as the relationship itself.

Like the Guys Group Intensive, our Private Couple's Intensive is a great option for anyone wanting to accelerate the healing process, because intensives take 4-6 months' worth of session work and condense it into 3 days. You will receive an assessment of your unique issues, 7-8 hours per day of instruction, exercises and tools to help you move forward, and a personalized recovery plan for yourself and/or your relationship. We provide you a shame-free environment to address your specific issues.

And, if you choose a Private Couple's Intensive, we want you to know that partners are always treated with respect, compassion, and validation for the pain that their partner's issues have caused them. As a partner, you will never be blamed or asked to take any responsibility for your partner's choices. Also, if desired, we have full disclosure and polygraph services available.

Learn more or sign up for a Private Couple's Intensive today

www.MyBecomingWell.com

Books and Courses

Moving Couples from Shattered to Strong

REBUILDING TRUST

A Couple's Guide to Healing After Betrayal

MATT BURTON
LAURA BURTON

www.MyBecomingWell.com

Books and Courses

Moving Couples from Shattered to Strong

REBUILDING TRUST FOR CHRISTIANS

A Couple's Guide to Healing After Betrayal

MATT BURTON
LAURA BURTON

www.MyBecomingWell.com

Books and Courses

Moving Partners from Shattered to Strong

Mending After Betrayal

BOOK AND WORKBOOK

LAURA BURTON

www.MyBecomingWell.com

Books and Courses

Moving Partners from Shattered to Strong

Mending After Betrayal

BOOK AND WORKBOOK FOR CHRISTIANS

LAURA BURTON

www.MyBecomingWell.com

Books and Courses

www.MyBecomingWell.com

Books and Courses

www.MyBecomingWell.com

Books and Courses

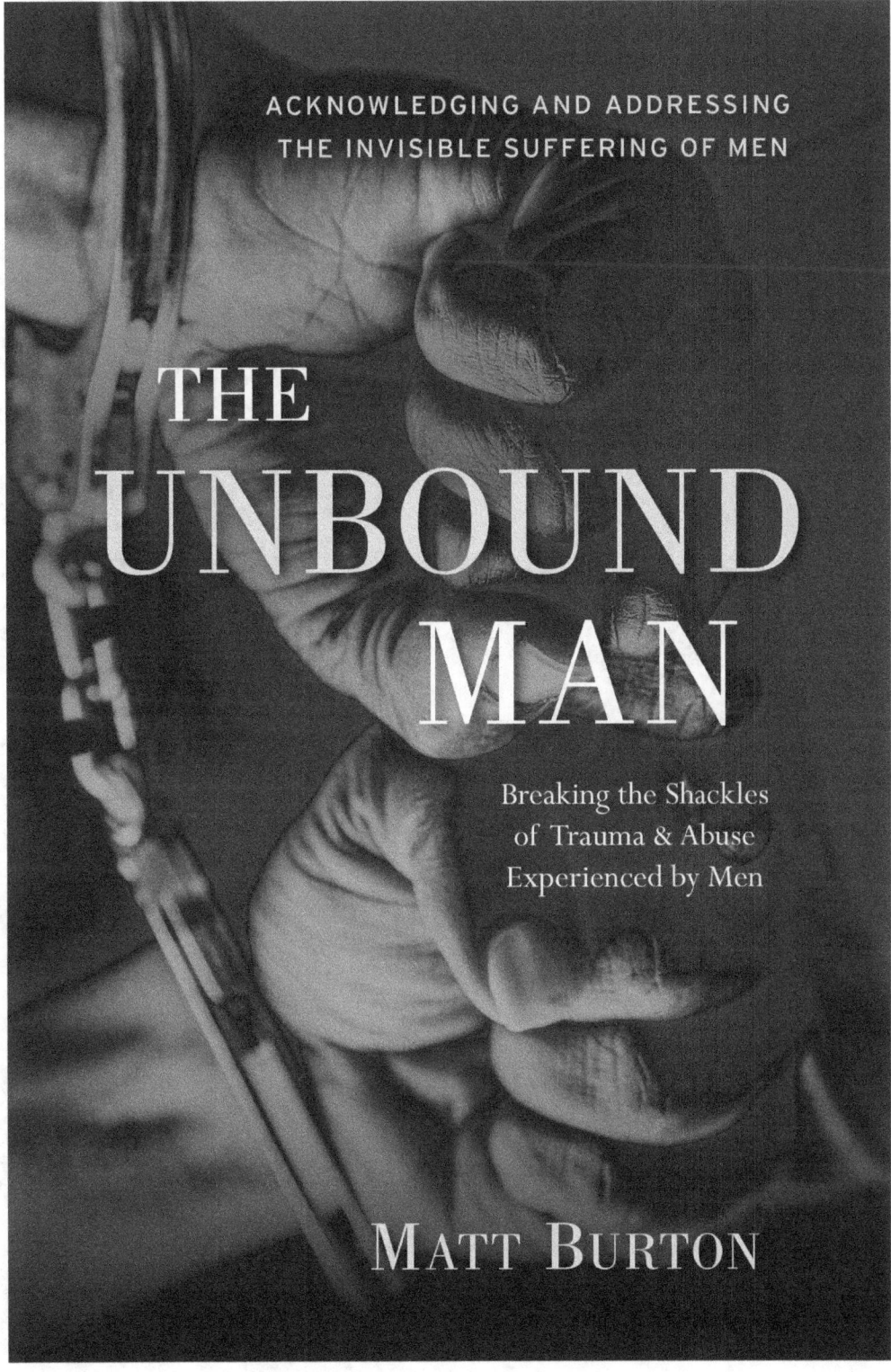

www.MyBecomingWell.com

Books and Courses

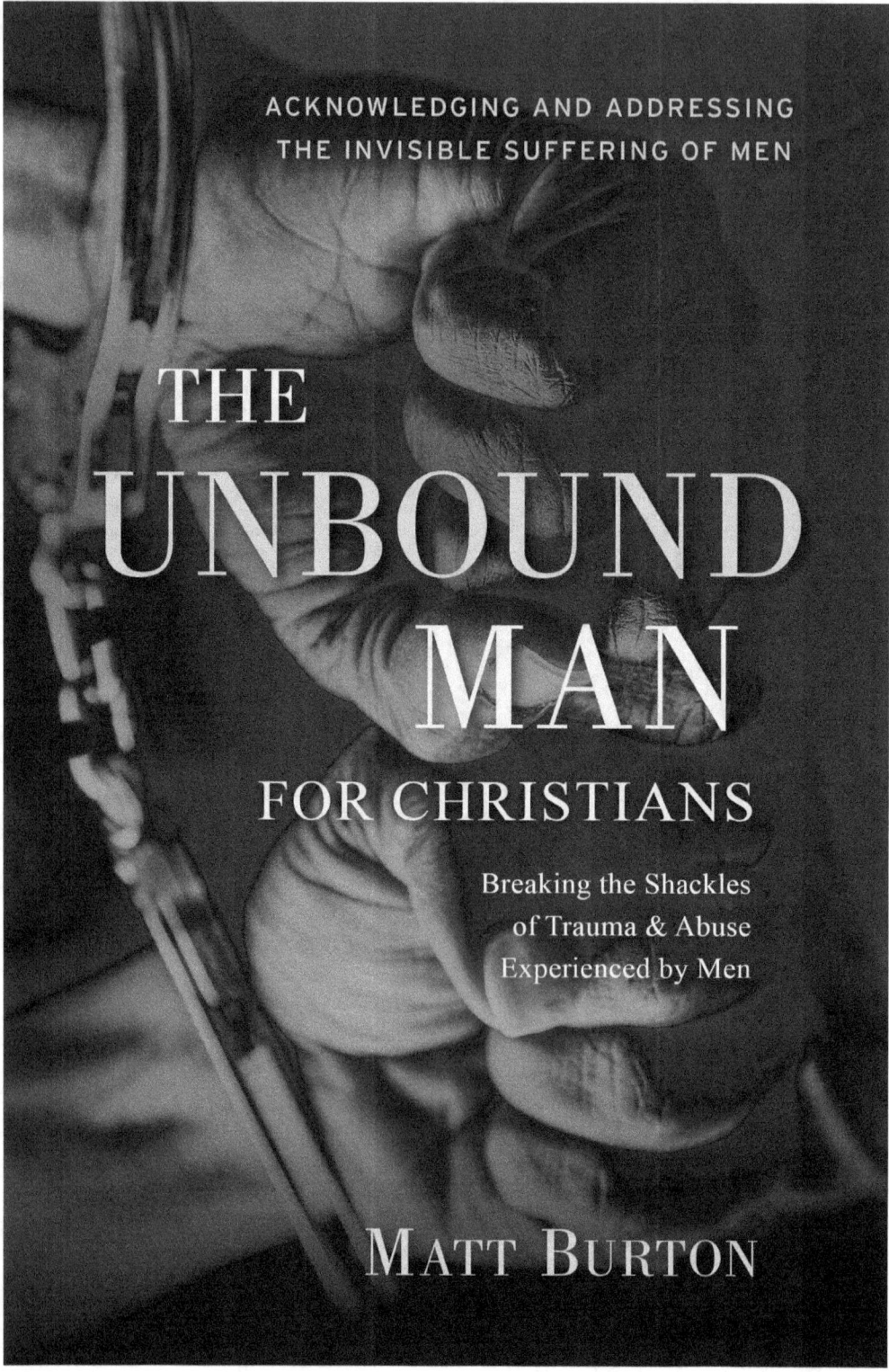

www.MyBecomingWell.com

Books and Courses

www.MyBecomingWell.com

Connect with Us

 www.facebook.com/mybecomingwell

 Becoming Well (@mybecomingwell)

 Becoming Well (@mybecomingwell)

 www.mybecomingwell.com

 info@mybecomingwell.com

 520-355-5322

www.ingramcontent.com/pod-product-compliance
Lightning Source LLC
LaVergne TN
LVHW081547070526
838199LV00061B/4243